THE ARYA SAMAJ MOVEMENT IN SOUTH AFRICA

THE ARYA SAMAJ MOVEMENT IN SOUTH AFRICA

Dr. Thillayvel Naidoo

MOTILAL BANARSIDASS PUBLISHERS
PRIVATE LIMITED • DELHI

First Edition: Delhi, 1992

ISBN: 81 208-0769-3

Also available at:
MOTILAL BANARSIDASS
41 U.A. Bungalow Road, Jawahar Nagar, Delhi 110 007
120 Royapettah High Road, Mylapore, Madras 600 004
16 St. Mark's Road, Bangalore 560 001
Ashok Rajpath, Patna 800 004
Chowk, Varanasi 221 001

PRINTED IN INDIA

BY JAINENDRA PRAKASH JAIN AT SHRI JAINENDRA PRESS,
A-45 NARAINA INDUSTRIAL AREA, PHASE I, NEW DELHI 110 028
AND PUBLISHED BY NARENDRA PRAKASH JAIN FOR MOTILAL
BANARSIDASS PUBLISHERS PVT. LTD., BUNGALOW ROAD,
JAWAHAR NAGAR, DELHI 110 007

Foreword

It is my pleasure and privilege to introduce the book "Arya Samaj Movement in South Africa" to the general public. It deals with the birth, development, progress and achievements of Arya Samaj in that country. Actually, the history of Arya Samaj Movement in South Africa is the history of emigrant Indians, particularly Hindus, who had gone and settled there during the last century.

The system of indentured labour took Indians in large numbers to the new British colonies established in many parts of the world, including South Africa, where the first contingent had landed in the year 1860. Later on, others also followed as free Indians and formed the core of Indian traders in that country. The Hindu migrants belonged both to orthodox Hindu faith (Sanātan Dharma) and the reformist Arya Samaj.

The sapling of Vedic Religion and culture, brought from India by the early settlers, in course of time grew into a formidable banayan tree, fostered by many Aryan missionaries from India who visited South Africa from time to time. Today, a good many benevolent institutions are working there, under the aegis of the Arya Samaj. Shri Naidoo has taken pains to put on record the history of the life and achievements of Arya Samaj in the socio-economic field of South Africa against the wider back-drop of Vedic religion and its impact on people in other countries.

I am sure, the book will provide a useful and authentic information about the Arya Samaj and its achievements in South Africa.

SWAMI ANAND BODH SARASWATI
President
Sarvadeshik Arya Pratinidhi Sabha

New Delhi
Dated 21st May 90

CONTENTS

TO

My Parents
Brothers and Sisters
whose love and encouragement
made this work possible

SECTION ONE

INTRODUCTION

Introduction

SUBJECT OF STUDY: THE ARYA SAMAJ

A STUDY OF the history of Hinduism in India reveals ironically its strange indifference to history. Hindu religious thought seems to have taken little account of the need for historical and social development. The establishment of Muslim-Mogul and later Christian-British rule in Hindustan seems to have become possible because of Hindu indifference to its own socio-political ideals in the light of its own religio-philosophical foundations. Among the vast number of other debilitating weaknesses inherent within it, were caste prejudices, religious superstition, innumerable social evils and, above all, the singular lack of a cohesive set of religiously inspired national and cultural ideals. This degeneration of Indian society, typified by mass poverty and social and religious corruption, made profound impacts upon people such as Swami Vivekananda and Swami Dayananda Sarasvati.

Swami Dayananda believed that India had degenerated, primarily because of her neglect of Vedic teachings and codes of conduct such as those inspired by the laws of Manu. His aim thus became the rejuvenation of Hinduism through the re-establishment of Vedic ideals. His work, *Satyartha Prakash*, in which he dealt critically with post-Mahābhārata ramifications of Hinduism and other faiths such as Buddhism, Jainism, Christianity and Islam is a comprehensive study. His thrust against other religions was directed chiefly against Islam and Christianity because of the aggressive intrusions of these faiths into Hindu society. The opponents he faced within Hinduism itself were, however, at times even more formidable. There were, firstly, the *pundits,* who exploited people's beliefs in superstition and idolatry and who advocated practices such as child marriage and enforced widowhood. Secondly, there were the brahmins (members of the privileged caste) and *sādhus* (wandering monks), whose pecuniary wants added to the confusion and worsening degeneration. To consolidate his work, Swami Dayananda formed a movement known as the Arya Samaj (Society of Noble People). The first centre of this institution was set up in Bombay in April 1875. His objective in founding the Samaj was to restructure Hindu society by eliminating social evils and re-introducing higher religious values among the people through numerous codes of behaviour. He stressed avoidance of rituals and theological complexities and in pursuit of his ideals he launched an action programme aimed at religious, social and educational reform.

He based religious reform on the bedrock of the Vedas, which alone he was convinced, held the key to arresting the decay into which Hinduism and Hindu culture had fallen. In the social field he stressed the eradication of practices such as idolatry, the caste system, untouchability and child marriage. These, he believed, had deflected Hinduism from its basic objectives. On the other hand, he advocated widow remarriage and the re-admission to Hinduism of those who had converted to other faiths. The *Śuddhī* movement started by him was one of the most revolutionary ever initiated within Hinduism and which later had historic significance for Hindu culture as a whole. For many centuries Hindus had denied admission into their fold, to members of other faiths, including those who had been drawn away from Hinduism and wished to reconvert. The impact of conversion to other faiths had made him realise that unless Hindus opened their doors to people of other faiths, Hinduism itself was endangered. The need to win back to its fold Hindus who had been converted to Islam and Christianity was therefore an important objective.

Politically, Swami Dayananda contended in 1875 that foreign rule was the main cause of India's degradation and poverty. He was therefore convinced that *swarāj* (home rule) was the only remedy for it and so he propagated the concept of *swadeśi* (the purchase and use of goods made only in India). His call for swarāj was a powerful motivating force for the Arya Samajists to join the national freedom struggle. However, Swami Dayananda will be remembered principally as an outstanding religious reformer. It was therefore natural that his followers, especially after the attainment of independence in 1947, paid particular attention to the spread of the Vedic religion as he taught it.

Swami Dayananda's teaching of Vedic religious ideals for twelve years culminated in the establishment of the Arya Samaj movement in Bombay on 10 April 1875.[1] Meeting under the direction of the Swami himself, a group of men and women, deeply dedicated to the Vedic ideals of religious and social upliftment of all peoples that made up Hindu society, committed themselves to the task. The organisation eventually became a world-wide Hindu movement and its impact upon South African Hinduism has been considerable with its growing influence continuing to affect many modes of worship found within the faith in South Africa.

The subject of this study is the Arya Samaj movement in South Africa, spearheaded by the Arya Pratinidhi Sabha of South Africa. The Arya Samaj is one of the most important religious movements to have been started, and due to its relative infancy, is confined largely to Natal. It has some forty-three affiliated units and affects the lives of several thousand people. This is however not intended to suggest that all Hindus in South Africa, nor even the majority, have come under its influence. This work does nevertheless suggest that it has had a very positive effect and engenders thereby some enlightened approaches to religious practice.

Aim of Study

The essential tasks in this study are:

Firstly, to examine the theological basis of the teachings propounded by Swami Dayananda and supported by the establishment and growth of the Arya Samaj movement in South Africa.

Secondly, to show how these teachings have influenced several aspects of Hindu life and thought in South Africa.

The study takes account of the cultural structure in which the Arya Samaj functions and the goals which provide the devotional frames of reference within the superordinate meaningfulness of the system formulated by Swami Dayananda and other preceptors within the movement.

The study concerns the nature of the empirical basis upon which elements within the system operate. While it is not intended to follow a cross-sectional approach as Hare[2] recommends, the study focuses on the cultural structure comprising goals and the aspirational frame of reference within the organismic structure per se. The institutional norms considered in the study regularise acceptable modes of aspiration towards those goals and values that systematise organic patterns of belief. The dynamic process of operation conceptualises the growth of the structure that has roots in holy scripture. For Dayananda these roots lie in Revelation. Talcot Parsons'[3] theory is that processes of socialisation and social control emanate from shared value systems as a means of functional necessity. Such necessity is therefore viewed within the context of the struggle for existence while a cultural basis enhances ultimate values that conform to the norm historicised by revelation.

Max Weber[4] saw religious ideas as the basis for religious action and ultimate values. These have been progressively formulated in the Samaj context as a new world meaning. Its postulates generate a religious meaning that conforms to the ultimate values it describes. The study attempts to understand how religious values are conceived and how responses to non-empirical concepts formulate the goals and approaches to those goals in addition to the integration of religious values that so develop.

METHOD OF APPROACH

The method of research employed in this work proceeded by way of study of the literature, the organisation itself both in India and South Africa, interviews with well-known Arya Samajists and attendance at various services and meetings of the various administrative bodies of the organisation.

The writer, apart from his position on the staff of the University of Durban-Westville, where he lectures on Hinduism, is also deeply interested in the work of several Hindu organisations in the country. His association with them enhanced contact with the Arya Pratinidhi Sabha. His friendship with its members made discussion on many matters of relevance easy and educative. Discussion on the concepts, modes of worship and religious beliefs obtaining within the Arya Samaj was at all times informative.

The approach was that of a participant observer in all Arya Samaj functions that he had the opportunity of attending in South Africa and India. This resulted in his being accepted within the movement as a participating member, a position commodious to the study. The writer was in a position to maintain sufficient distance however to make objective observations and examination of the practices in relation to the theological position and beliefs of participating members. Different degrees of understanding, honesty and sincerity of approach were encountered, underlined by the fact that religious convictions were volatile and fluid, and members displayed varying degrees of appreciation of theological concepts. This gave rise to several difficulties aggravated by the fact that serious study of Arya Samaj teachings and formulation of constructive ideas on many facets of life was usually stifled due to the lack of sufficient study by members of the organisation. Discussion had necessarily to follow a hampered course. These difficulties were, however, eventually minimised with the help of constructive suggestions offered by associates and colleagues. In time, the study became pleasant and information was gathered with relative ease and convenience.

Literary Sources

Most of the literary sources consulted during the course of the study were published in India. The Arya Pratinidhi Sabha, largely through its own subsidiary organisation, the Veda Niketan, has been responsible for a few publications of its own, but these were very inadequate for this study. It has produced numerous pamphlets on the occasion of various festivals, including the celebration of special occasions such as the "silver" and "golden" jubilees of its existence, for which souvenir-brochures were produced. The rest of the material consulted comprised books produced by scholars in India and occasional newspaper and magazine articles formed supportive sources.

Institutional Development

The Arya Pratinidhi Sabha, established in 1925, is the parent organisation to which are affiliated several subsidiary institutions. This thesis is concerned with the most important of these. Arya Samaj institutions in India were visited with the intention of comparing the quality of practice and service adhered to in South Africa under Indian directives. Visits were paid to the Arya Samaj headquarters at New Delhi, the Gurukul Kangri near Haridwar, the institution in Bombay where the movement had its birth and a few of the others connected with the larger movement in that country. It was therefore possible to see at first hand the inner workings of the entire organisation and thereby to gain the insight necessary to see the South African subsidiary in operation. The links that exist between the Sabha in South Africa and India and with other Arya Samaj organisations elsewhere are not formal. This enables each national organisation to pursue its objectives with some freedom at a pace suited to local conditions. Official rules and regulations have been reduced to a minimum and control by the mother institution is now by agreement rather than official or regulatory.

Personal Interviews

The writer interviewed two groups of people within the Arya Samaj movement and one group outside it. In this way it was possible to gauge opposing shades of view. In the chapter entitled "Reception and Dialogue" in the third section of this study the arguments against many of the teachings of the Arya Samaj are outlined. These agreements helped the writer to formulate thinking in the wider sphere, in movements that do not support the strictly non-conformist views of the Arya Samaj. The interviews in South Africa were prolonged and extensive and much information was gathered thereby on Arya Samaj principles as they exist within the local organisation. Members had the opportunity of discussing their beliefs frankly, with the result that elucidation of problems was clear, invigorating and beneficial. In India the interviews had necessarily to be short and deliberate. Much insight was gained on the deep interest that exists in the work of Swami Dayananda among many persons and some attempt has been made to assess this interest and its value for Hinduism generally.

In South Africa, interviews were held in four main centres, Durban, Pietermaritzburg, Johannesburg and Port Elizabeth. Six of the interviewees were ex-students of the Arya Samaj Gurukuls in Navsari, Baroda and Haridwar. Several people in the Gujarati speaking community who were inspired by Arya Samaj ideals sent their sons and daughters to India to receive primary and secondary school education there. Interviews with these students were very elucidating and added considerably to the weight of this study.

CONCLUSION

In concluding this introduction to the study, attention is drawn to the way in which the study progressed. The second chapter has of necessity to be expository. It reflects on the most important biographical details of Swami Dayananda's life. Like so many other teachers these details have some bearing on his theology and form a basis upon which the Arya Samaj movement built its philosophical edifice. Swami Dayananda indicated clearly his own understanding of religion and its true function and purpose for man. He formulated a programme of action for the social and cultural upliftment of his people. Environmental, socio-political and to a lesser extent historical influences appear to have considerable bearing on the theological foundations of his movement.

Social change is generated within a structural balance, says Weber. Shifts within the structure of interaction appear, in the case of the Hindu community in South Africa, to be sufficiently powerful to be the cause of the modification intended through purposeful motivation. The realignment in tendencies appears to all intents and purposes, to be a favourable reassertion of the principles that initiated the first shift towards the Arya Samaj view of reality. The effect upon Hindu society is not only seen to be reflective of its capacity for innovation and structural change but more deeply of its ability to reassert structural changes that would promote the growth and development of higher motives and values.

REFERENCES

1. Rolland, Romain, *The Life of Ramakrishna,* Advaita Ashrama, Calcutta, 1970, p 135.

2. Hare, A.P., *Handbook of Small Group Research*, Free Press, Glencoe,Illinois, 1952, p 11.

3. Parsons, Talcott, *Structure and Process in Modern Societies,* Free Press, Glencoe, Illinois, 1960.

4. Weber, Max, *The Theory of Social and Economic Organisation,* Tr. Henderson, A.M. and Parsons, T., Oxford University Press, 1947.

SECTION TWO

SWAMI DAYANANDA AND THE INDIAN SITUATION

Introduction

WE BEGIN our study with an analysis of the roots from which germinated the ideas for the Arya Samaj movement. The seeds of religious encounter were contained in Swami Dayananda's own life experience, which formed the central pivot around which his spiritual growth revolved. It was however his deep interest in the Vedas which formed the core of his religious life. The Vedas he brought to life again after their confinement to the dim obscurity to which they had been relegated by Indian negligence.

We begin our study with a consideration of the biographical details that had much bearing on the formation of the movement. The study will consider therefore not only the theological implications of the teachings, but also their strong influence on the sociological extension upon which Swami Dayananda concentrated so much of his attention. Reinhold Niebuhr's[1] contention that religion is continually renewed out of the incongruous situation of man is affirmed in the disorder and incoherence of life that received Dayananda's attention.

Swami Dayananda's approach has obvious functional overtones. To be sure his difficulties mounted with the theological demands of his approach forcing upon him a not inconsiderable evaluative stance. For him religion at its simplest was seen as a system of beliefs and practices and these he placed within the context of human struggle and the need to know their ultimate value.

Joachim Wach[2] holds that religion is characterised by at least three universal expressions: the theoretical, constituting its system of beliefs, the practical, in which a system of worship evolves, and the sociological, in which social relationships are enhanced. Arya Samajist approaches were able to provide the basic elements and religious tendencies which clearly agree with Wach's theory. Although the first of these expressions, the system of beliefs, falls naturally into the category which Dayananda appeared to have considered the heart of religion, other evidence seems to suggest that religion as worship and religion as a system of social relationships may be basic, with belief being supportive to his system of worship.

Following on Dayananda's functional approach, this study will consider not the nature of the beliefs within the movement, but the nature of the approaches to those beliefs. Justification for this arises, despite the diversity of beliefs even within a single homogeneous system, from the assumption that many forms represent different attempts to deal with the same problem. Throughout the study we are reminded of the implications of the revolution in religious behaviour which influenced among many a new brand of nationalism. The traditional religion of Indian society was clearly losing some of its appeal. So the new faith had to be recast into that which replaced old and obsolete religious practices with a new set of religious ideals.

REFERENCES

1. Niebuhr, R., *The Nature and Destiny of Man*, Charles Scribner, New York, 1964.
2. Wach, J., *Sociology of Religion*, Kegan Paul, Trench, Trabner and Co., London, 1947.

CHAPTER 1

Life of Swami Dayananda Sarasvati (1825-1883)

SWAMI DAYANANDA was born at Tankara in the Indian province of Gujarat in 1825[1]. His education commenced when he was five years old. When he reached the age of eight, he was invested with the sacred thread (*Yajñopavīta Saṁskāra*), as was customary for a Brahmin child, whereby he was initiated into the *Sandhyā* and *Upāsanā* sacraments[2]. It was soon after this that his spiritual calling became manifest and he began to reveal strong tendencies of adoration of Lord Śiva. At the age of ten he began to observe rigorous fasts, listen to *Kāthās* (stories) and keep long vigils during many nights of prayer. He was a precocious student and learning came easily to him. At the age of fourteen he had committed to memory the whole of the *Yajur Veda Saṁhitā*, some portions of the remaining three Vedas and some minor works of Sanskrit grammar. He however understood very little of what he could repeat.

It was at this age too that he received the first of two great shocks that were to make such a deep impression upon him and revolutionise his entire approach to spiritual matters.[3] As a young person, he was deeply imbued with the idea of God's Revelation. Spiritual discipline was, however, necessary and for a Śaivite family the fast and ceremonial vigil over the festival of Śivarātri was one of the most austere. The entire night is observed as a night of prayer and the deity in the temple is worshipped in four stages. One of the rules of the ceremony is that the devotee who observes the fast must remain awake the whole night; otherwise the observance is meaningless. During one such vigil the first quarter of the night passed off well; during the second stage the proceedings became less animated but the majority of the people continued with the rite. During the third quarter most of the devotees were unable to resist sleep.

When virtually all the other devotees, including the priests, were unable to maintain the vigil and fell asleep, Dayananda had the first of several deeply disturbing experiences. A mouse crept out of its hole and walked over the image of Śiva to help itself to the food offerings which had been brought by the worshippers. For many moments the boy watched in horror as the little creature pranced from food item to food item. He sat stupefied as he watched the lowly creature desecrate the image, the food offerings and the sacred ceremony with its unholy presence.

The boy Moolshankar thought long and intently over the incident, as the seriousness of it had a traumatic impact upon him. So deeply was he affected by it that he resolved, subsequent to many deeply searching questions that raced through his precocious mind, to ponder over many of the religious problems he knew others of his temperament faced. The point of his concern lay with the worship of an idol. That it could be revered as a physical representation of the Most High at one moment and be desecrated by vermin at the next was not a spiritual experience of any joy, not even for one of such deep commitment as he. The torment was brutal. It was then that the future religious leader received his call from God in which he was exhorted to study the Vedas and be spiritually enriched in the knowledge and wisdom of those scriptures. The call directed him to a commitment of study and religious discipline which would later be followed by his leading many of his countrymen to a new direction in religious thinking. "Dayananda's soul had heard the words and took in the inspiration in a vague, half-conscious fashion to be realised and worked out in the gradually increasing enlightenment of later years."[4]

For Dayananda the torment was deep and agonising. A dialogue with his father, a deeply committed Śaivite Brahmin, failed to resolve his problem. The solution offered was at best, for him, a travesty of even the simplest reasoning on such matters. If a mouse could take such liberties with a revered image of the Lord, how does He offer protection to Himself, let alone to others? It appeared to him utterly impossible to reach the living omnipotent Lord through the medium of an idol made of stone. Because his faith in idol-worship had been badly shaken, he resolved to search out God and, if possible, meet Him face to face. He thus devoted himself to his studies, determined to solve through pure reason many of the problems he encountered in interpreting correctly the true meaning of holy scripture.[5]

Two years later Dayananda received a second great shock. His young sister died after a very short and sudden illness. The incident brought home to him the cold callousness of death and his resolve became one of adamantine search for Truth in which the meaning of life, and so death, could become clear to him.

He gave up all thoughts of marriage and was able, after much discussion with his parents, to temporarily delay this for some time. However, after a year he was informed of their intention to prepare for his wedding, against which he had much personal resolve. He moved to another village as a temporary solution, in the hope that the time could be usefully spent in studies. His decision never to marry was conveyed to his parents who disregarded his wishes and prepared for his wedding. Moolshankar's pre-occupation with spiritual matters forced him into a strong desire to forego entry into *gṛhastha-āśrama*, the householder's station in life. His admiration and love for many great teachers of earlier years forced him to resolve against marriage, hoping thereby to follow in the paths of religious investigation they took. He chose to leave home, perhaps never to return.

During the flight from his home he arrived at the house of a distinguished student of scripture named Lala Bhagat who had as permanent guests numerous ochre-clad students who had dedicated themselves to a religious life. One of the brahmacārins conferred upon him the privilege of the Order to which they belonged and named him Shuddha-Chaitanya (Pure Minded). His obvious flair for leading the life of a renunciant by wearing the ochre robe and carrying a beggar's gourd enabled him to join the band of monks and dedicate himself to study and religious discipline. However, he was located by his father who had set out after him. His second attempt at leaving home forced him to wander incognito until he was safely out of the reach of his parents.

Swami Dayananda had a strong desire to become a monk. With the assistance of a learned *pundit* in the district, he persuaded Swami Purnananda Sarasvati to initiate him into the holy order of *Sannyāsa*. The important ceremony took place and soon the young Moolshankar, alias Shuddha-Chaitanya, became the monk renunciant Swami Dayananda of the Sarasvati Order in his twenty-fourth year. A life of total independence, dedication and study followed which enabled him to undergo rigorous religious disciplines and then to preach the message of the Vedas to millions of his own countrymen.

His wanderings thereafter became more purposeful. He met Swami Yogananda and studied with him all aspects of Yoga Philosophy and its disciplines. He later went to Krishna Shastri at

Cinor and continued his studies of Sanskrit grammar. He then joined another *pundit* with whom he continued his studies of the Vedas. He joined two yogis named Jwalananda Puri and Shivananda Giri to continue his studies of Yoga.[6] He always expressed his gratitude to those two teachers for all he had learnt from them. He continued his wanderings and meetings with many of the wise and competent teachers in several parts of the country from Mount Abu to Rishikesh and Haridwar. He also learnt something about the Tantras, a branch of learning that fell into disrepute because of the nature of its practices. His travels in the country brought him to the famous pilgrim centres of Jośhimaṭha and Badrinārāyan. His disappointment at not meeting any learned monks drove him further on in his search. At this time his greatest desire was to associate with all the learned men he could find for the purposes of learning as much as he could from them. During these travels he had to endure many hardships. There was little food to be had, his clothes were scanty and he seldom found any comfortable place for rest or lodging. At times he was forced to eat ice to stave off thirst and hunger. When attempting to cross the icy waters of the Alakanandā River, filled as it was with rocks and stones, he encountered many difficulties. "His feet were wounded and bleeding and utterly dismembered with cold and he felt like one in a state of stupefaction."[7]

Swami Dayananda continued his journey with renewed earnestness. Despite the difficulties his search continued. During this part of his wanderings as a *Parivrājaka* (wandering monk) he studied and practised austerities in order to prepare himself for the great tasks that lay ahead. His wanderings led him to many remote areas of the country. On one occasion he came across a corpse being carried along a river by a strong current. Dayananda had with him several books on physiology and anatomy. To widen his knowledge he cut up the corpse and examined it in every detail. Needless to say his interest in the subject was considerably enhanced.

In 1856, Swami Dayananda was still walking the country visiting holy cities and pilgrim centres, meeting with and talking to many students of Vedic learning. In 1859, one of the more momentous events of his life occurred at Mathura. Here, he met the man who was to make a profound contribution to his spiritual and intellectual development. Dayananda was accepted as a student by Swami Virajananda and a long and close association between the two religious scientists commenced. At the time of their meeting there was great famine and hardship in the area. His firm resolve to dedicate his life to study at such a time won the hearts of his Guru and several friends in the area who agreed to help him in every possible way.[8]

Few men toiled, laboured and sacrificed as Dayananda did.[9] Every act of his mind and will became from then on a legacy to the belief that only the purest and most sublime of Vedic teachings had to become the basis of his life, the very soul of spiritual endeavour in his native land. The first five years of his ministry (1863-1868) as teacher and reformer were somewhat uneventful. Much of this time was spent in travelling around India visiting centres of pilgrimage and more specially meeting students and scholars well-versed in the various branches of Indian philosophical and religious literature. The Swami engaged in numerous discussions and disputations with people in every city, town and village he visited. In these discussions he levelled considerable criticism against many of the popular notions held by the people. He was particularly vociferous in his criticism of the Śrimad Bhāgavatam, a popular Pūraṇa which he regarded as immoral.[10] During this time he also met several British students and ministers of religion with whom he discussed at length many contentious matters that were popular among people at the time.

In November 1866, he arrived at a *durbār* in Agra with five friends and fellow students (*vidyārthīs*), anxious to spread his teachings and to engage in dialogue with others in the hope of convincing them of new ideas and approaches to religious matters. At the Kumbha Fair, Swami Dayananda had one of his saddest experiences. He had gone there with great hopes and had put all his energy into the work that had carried him thither but for all that, the fair left his spirits weighed down and depressed. He was appalled by the idolatry and the general lust after material wealth and pleasure that he saw around him. He grew more deeply affected at the thought that very much the same attitude pervaded the thinking and behaviour of many others in the rest of India. He then believed that India was leagued against herself and bent on self-destruction. It was then that he felt moments of great despair; but instead of wilting under these burdens he firmly resolved to continue. "All that I need", he said, "is more force, moral and spiritual force, which will come through spiritual discipline."[11]

He was well aware of the value of winning young men over to the Truth as he understood it. This enthusiasm, however, attracted many young men who proved to be villains and mischief makers who made several attempts on his life. On more than one occasion he was given poison, but he saved himself by resort to adequate measures of medication and cure. He was, however, generally all-forgiving and even those who on many occasions chose to heap contempt upon him were usually won over by love and became some of his closest friends. Their admiration for him came as a result of his own austere living and frugal habits. For example, he sought, even on extremely cold nights, no better bed than a heap of straw or paddy husks. Defying sickness of every kind, he lived on meagre resources, dedicated to the task he had taken upon himself: that of spreading Vedic truth in its purest form.

In 1868 Swami Dayananda resolved to bring order into his work and to prepare for the establishment of educational institutions through which his message could be put to practical effect. He concluded that schools had to be established where religion could be taught. His appeal to friends and associates and the public at large drew favourable response. One enthusiastic supporter was Panna Lal Seth, who was at the time working on the construction of a *Śivālaya* (*Śiva* Temple) and decided immediately to incorporate into it a pāṭhśālā (school). This was followed by the establishment of another pāṭhśālā two years later at Kasganj and a third at Mirzapur in the same year. A fourth was established at Chhalesar, at the request of Thakur Singh. A characteristic of all the pāṭhśālās established by the Swami was that for the first time some order was introduced into the general scheme of learning and each student gained valuable knowledge on the general aims of study at these institutions. The rules that were enforced were very strictly followed and considerable measure of order was maintained for Vedic study. However, the schools were never really successful. The Swami had little alternative but to close them down after a short while having admitted to failure in achieving his original aims.[12]

Swami Dayananda's dedication continued unabated, however, and he embarked upon a new programme of teaching and preaching in which one of the main concerns was the condemnation of old superstitious practices, particularly, implicit belief in the *Bhagavata* better known as *Śrimad Bhāgavatam*. It is somewhat ironical that an Indian Swami such as Dayananda should have held such deep resentment for a work which many Hindus saw as the very foundation of their religious existence.

Aldous Huxley says of the work: "It expresses the essence of Indian religion almost as forcefully as does the *Bhagavad Gītā*." Christopher

Isherwood considers it "one of the great religious classics of the world."[13]

The Arya Samaj movement today faces the onerous task of having to explain its rejection of this work while a modern Hindu religious movement (Iskcon) known worldwide for its buoyant propagation of the message of Śri Kṛṣṇa uses the very *Bhāgavatam* as its canonical Scripture.[14] Translations of this work now run into several volumes and abridged versions are sold in many countries and in several Indian and European languages.

The Swami participated in another debate at the town of Soron near Karnavas, where he succeeded in converting several people of the Chakarankit faith to the Vedic religion. His disputations with learned *pundits* often ended in victory for him. He repudiated idolatry on the authority of the Vedas and exposed the Bhāgavata to ridicule. Other learned *pundits* were amazed at his attitude because few people before him had ever dared to oppose the teachings of the Purāṇas, a set of scriptures that had been popular in India for many centuries. His exhortations led people to consign *śāligrāms, kaṇṭhis* and *tilakas* to rivers, thus dispensing with so-called aids to spiritual growth and taking recourse to intelligent study and the practice of religious discipline. His six-month stay at Soron was an important feature of his travels and teaching. He taught people to recite the *Gāyatrī* and to use its recitation as the basis of meditation.

Although the Swami faced considerable opposition from orthodoxy, his resolute and fearless stand brought him many admirers. At a fair in Kasganj some people, sympathetic to his message, sought his favour to show some leniency towards idol worship. He was, however, adamant: "The things of the world which yield pleasure to you, have no charm for me. To me there is pleasure in the contemplation and adoration of God alone and in carrying out His commandments. I shall work with the one, sole objective of disseminating true Vedic knowledge."[15] His open challenge to anyone to deny that the ancient religion of the Aryans as taught in the Vedas, was the purest and noblest went unheeded and his popularity and success began to make an impression upon the society he chose to serve, transform and love with such dedication.[16]

Swami Dayananda's resolute stand against idolatry was interpreted by some as over-enthusiastic zeal, making far too great an impact upon a religious tradition that went back many centuries. He naturally aroused the ire of people such as Pandit Siri Gopal and others of Farrukhabad who reverted to the use of scripture to refute the stand taken by him.

Possibly the most vehement criticism that could be levelled against Swami Dayananda was his refusal to compromise. His obvious repugnance for "idol-worship" aroused the indignation of many and the more erstwhile among them became very resentful of his open hostility. His refusal to adopt a more tactful strategy of constructive influence failed to earn him the following he could possibly have got otherwise.

The speed at which he went from village to village and town to town in northern India resulted in his failure to reap greater rewards for the movement. He attempted too much too quickly, with the result that much time was lost in opposing people and being opposed by those who had little real interest in reforming themselves, whereas he could have used his time to winning friends and maintaining their support.

Unlike Swami Vivekananda, who adopted a totally different stance that involved patient study, travel throughout the country meeting people and so winning friends and laying proper foundations for the enormous tasks he had, Swami Dayananda was openly hostile to people on many occasions and often adopted totally uncompromising attitudes. His open and frank claims and decisions as to his purpose often left him open to attack. Had his approach been more gentle and sober, first winning the confidence of friends and supporters, he would almost certainly have achieved greater success.

The *Śāstrārtha* held at Kanpur, which attracted thousands of people, was one of the most momentous meetings ever held by him.[17] The subject of discussion was idolatry and, as was expected, Pandit Haldar Ojha engaged him in debate. The Swami's contention was that the Vedas never supported idol worship as such. The pundit's response was: "If the Vedas do not enjoin idol worship where do they condemn it?" There is no evidence that the Swami had any rejoinder to this.

The Swami's zeal, however, in talking to people and writing newspaper articles and pamphlets received considerable support. Though opposition to his ideas was at first formidable he penetrated through to large groups of people and in time signs of success became discernible. The editorial in a local newspaper at Sholapur in July 1869 spoke highly of the Swami's influence and insight, and the religious rejuvenation he was able to invoke among many communities.[18]

On 23 October 1869, Kashi had to face the onslaught of one of India's great sons of sincere resolve. The Swami's fearless resolution to oppose idolatry in any form aroused the wrath of many learned *pundits* including the Maharaja of Kashi, a keen student and one always disposed to ensuring that discussions with him were kept within the limits of reasonable rapport. The Kashi *Śāstrārtha* was unique in that the *pundits* chose to ascertain the source of the information on which Swami Dayananda based his contentions. It was unique also because Swami Dayananda encountered some of India's most learned *pundits* and other scholars such as Swami Vishuddhananda, who proved to be a formidable opponent. Swami Dayananda's views were not easily acceptable. While it appeared that he was deeply concerned about the form of worship and religious affiliation that people accepted, he could do very little to convince them of the need for reform and change. His objective was to transform Hindu society to a point where it no longer accepted debased schools of philosophy, the Purāṇas, caste and idolatry. His single aim was that Hindus would revert "back to the Vedas", when only one God would be adored, the Vedas studied and the sacrifice of *homa* be performed for the benefit of all, irrespective of caste or station of life.[19]

In the 1860s the Brahmo Samaj was at the height of its power. Many of its leading members took a keen interest in Swami Dayananda in the hope that they might be able to persuade him to join their movement. In the discussion that took place between them they discovered some irreconcilable differences of viewpoint on several matters. His uncompromising stand on the authority of the Vedas and several other issues related to the importance of some scriptural texts naturally brought much disagreement with the Brahmos at Calcutta. His love for Sanskrit proved to be somewhat burdensome as many of its associates preferred to speak in Hindi and Bengali. His stay there however proved interesting and discussion sometimes resulted in very valuable exchange of ideas. He had a meeting with Śri Ramakrishna which was brief and no major exchange of ideas occurred between them.[20] His attempt to establish Vedic schools proved futile and he left Calcutta in April 1873 somewhat disappointed.

His arrival in Bihar was marked by the usual interest aroused among large groups of people. Although many people felt much sympathy for his work and ideas this was always overshadowed by opposition from *pundits* who vehemently held fast to views that differed radically from his. The discussions on caste and idolatry were characterised by vehemence, vituperation and calumny. Most hurled abuses at him and he had to withstand insults and abuse at every turn. So deeply was he committed to his own viewpoint that whenever an opportunity arose to speak he did so at great length, sometimes in lectures lasting several hours. His audiences, though moved and convinced of the quality of his reasoning, found it difficult, if asked, to change radically after a lifetime of commitment to a traditional pattern of belief.

In July 1874, in Allahabad, Swami Dayananda was confronted by a *śāstri* who wished to know why his meetings sometimes raised such commotion. The Swami's reply underlined the tasks he had set himself and proved to many his firm conviction that a purpose had to be fulfilled. He contended that as so many *pundits* promulgated ideas that often emerged as trickery and deceit in the name of religion, he had come to defend the eternal principles of truth and justice and, above all, introduce a measure of sanity into the religion he loved and wished so dearly to see return to its pristine form in the land of its birth.

In September 1883 Swami Dayananda left Jodhpur where he had been heavily engaged in preaching among the people who included the Mahārājā of the principality. On the 29th of the month the Swami realised during the night that he was becoming very ill—this after drinking a glass of milk as he had always done. The pains became violent and it soon became evident that he had been poisoned. It was decided to remove him to Ajmer where doctors would be able to administer more suitable medication than was available at Jodhpur. His arrival in Ajmer was too late, however; the doctors were able to do very little for him, and the great Swami Dayananda passed away on Dīpāvali day in October 1883.

REFERENCES

1. Singh, B.C., *Life and Teachings of Swami Dayananda*, Jan Gyan Prakashan, New Delhi, 1871.
2. Singh, B.C., *Ibid*, p. 2.

3. Rolland, R., *The Life of Ramakrishna*, Advaita Ashrama, Calcutta, 1970, p. 128.
4. Singh, B.C., *Ibid*, p. 4.
5. Sarda, H.B., *Life of Dayanand Saraswati*, Vedic Yantralaya, Ajmer, 1946, p. 6.
6. Sarda, H.B., *Ibid*, p. 9.
7. Jnani, Pandit K., *The Inner Man*, p. 9.
8. Shastri, V., *The Arya Samaj*, Sarvadeshik Arya Pratinidhi Sabha, Delhi, 1967.
9. Rolland R., *Ibid*, p. 131.
10. Jordens, J.T.F., *Dayananda Sarasvati: His Life and Ideas*, p. 60.
11. Mal, Bahadur, *Dayananda: A Study in Hinduism*, p. 47.
12. Shastri, V., *Ibid*, p. 17.
13. Prabhavananda, S., *The Wisdom of God*. Capricorn Books, New York, 1968.
14. Prabhupada, S., *Śrimad Bhagavatam*, Bhakti Vedanta Book Trust, Los Angeles, 1977.
15. Aurobindo, S., *Bankim, Tilak, Dayananda*, Śri Aurobindo Ashram, Pondicherry, 1970.
16. Rolland, R., *Ibid*, p. 132.
17. Sarda, H.B., *Ibid*, p. 63.
18. Singh, B.C., *Ibid*, p. 59.
19. Satyaprakash, S., *Dayananda's Vedic Philosophy*, Dayanand Sansthan, Delhi, 1975.
20. Rolland, R., *Ibid*, p. 134.

CHAPTER 2

Swami Dayananda's Work for Indian Social and Religious Upliftment

THE SOCIAL CONDITIONS that prevail in India today are well-known. It is described as one of the third world countries with a gross national product that once made it one of the poorest nations on earth. However much economic advances are made through rapid industrialisation, the country's social and economic problems dominate every segment of her national life. At the time of Swami Dayananda's birth, India's social, economic, political and religio-cultural problems were deeply disturbing features of the nation's development. The general state of degeneration to which the country had fallen was often ascribed to the hundreds of years of neglect through nebulousness and foreign domination that had reduced the country to near ruin in almost every sphere of her national life. While most people were aware of these conditions and were able to do very little about them, it was necessary for a man of extraordinary talent to be born, to help eradicate the scourge of neglect in ways he believed possible or necessary. One suggestion was that Swami Dayananda's attempt at religious generation was at least one genius necessary for a many-sided contribution to the massive effort.[1]

Swami Dayananda's entire life was dedicated to the highest ideals of personal religious, and so national religious, integrity. His life was thus a deeply moving spiritual odyssey with almost every moment of it drawn to an undaunted yearning for expression of only the purest of spiritual ideals. The emotional disturbances at the sight of India's poverty and human degradation and its ignorance of more enlightened approaches to religious matters were experiences reserved only for those endowed with a saintly capacity for great suffering. The work done by Swami Dayananda was obviously the result of his total dedication, with fanatical zeal, to an ideal of lasting transformation of Indian society. His task, it seems, was to purge society of its rampant evils; evils that he believed had no place in a land that built her history on the bedrock of Vedic truth.

ATTACK ON IDOLATRY

As a teacher, Swami Dayananda concentrated his efforts on preaching against idolatry in every form. The force of his attacks was seen in the Śāstrārthas which he held in every town and village in the northern expanse of the country. At Haridwar on 12th March 1867[2], he began his public denunciation of the evil practices within Hinduism by speaking out against idol worship. He was also opposed to one of the fundamental tenets of Vaiśnavite religion, the belief in the Avatāras of Viṣṇu.

It was at Śāstrārthas that he scored his greatest victories over opponents. His primary objective at these Śāstrārthas was to convince people of the need for a totally new approach to religion. A Śāstrārtha was traditionally held for the purpose of exegetical discussion and interpretation of the most important of Hindu scriptures. Swami Dayananda used Śāstrārthas as the means of his ministry. They were convened mainly for the purpose of refuting false claims in understanding scriptural texts, and to convince others that no scriptural injunction could be found for idol worship in any form.[3] Swami Dayananda held these Śāstrārthas in many parts of the country. It is beyond the scope of this work to discuss them all so we confine ourselves to a few of the most significant ones in order to consider the nature of the discussions and the success he achieved thereby.

THE *ŚĀSTRĀRTHA* AT HARIDWAR—FEBRUARY 1868

The primary task in this *Śāstrārtha* was to make clear to all that a new force had arisen on India's religious frontier to rid the country of its ignorance, superstition and corruption. Swami Dayananda said that the descendants of heroes, warriors, philosophers, statesmen and scholars were now grovelling in the dust of irreligion, deprived of political liberty and bound fast to superstition and mental slavery. He reminded his listeners of the glory their forefathers had won in every field of human activity, that they were strangers to their glorious heritage and were drifting away from truth, strength and happiness. Flying a flag of his own, proclaiming liberty and freedom from falsehood and superstition, he called on the people, through his passion for moral living, to renounce false beliefs, to accept the truth of the Vedas and to cast off the chains that stunted this growth and bound them to slavery.[4]

The Śāstrārtha underlined the Swami's conviction that worship of the impersonal Being was far more relevant and necessary and that all other forms of prayer were a travesty of true worship.[5] His belief arose from the fact that so often the Purāṇas were quoted by people for such practices as drinking, gambling, adultery, etc. and these he felt were the cause of the desecration in religious affairs that he saw everywhere.

THE ŚĀSTRĀRTHA AT FARRUKHABAD—MAY 1869

Whenever the Swami arrived at a town or village he invariably invited local *pundits* to a discussion at the Śāstrārtha he would convene to invoke interest among the local residents. The Śāstrārtha at Farrukhabad in May 1869 was one of the most acrimonious and bitterly contested discussions he engaged in. One of those present, Pandit Siri Gopal of the Meerut District, was an avowed exponent of Purāṇic thought and hence supported the system of worship that Swami Dayananda denounced.[6] The pundit's first argument arose from his belief that *pūjā* (ritual) was required to be performed. He quoted from *Manu Smṛti*, which declared that *pūjā* was due to the *Devatās* (deities) and was adamant that that system of worship was indispensable for all Hindus. The Swami's contention was that *pūjā* meant honouring or showing reverence and that in the verse quoted it meant nothing more than performing *Agnihotra* (fire sacrifice).[7] The discussion ended in a stalemate with neither person conceding that arguments both for and against were valid or acceptable. The Pandit put forward many arguments to support his contention that worship of stone images was a necessary part of worship. These were invariably obtained from the Purāṇas. In all discussions between Arya Samajists and Sanatanis the Purāṇas have featured prominently in support of image worship. Pandit Siri Gopal always quoted, in support of his contentions, Vedic passages that appeared to give some authority to the Purāṇas. On another occasion Pandit Haldar in a debate with Swami Dayananda cited the incident from the Mahābhārata in which a Bhīl (tribesman) was said to have made an image of Ācārya Droṇa and worshipped it.[8] Swami Dayananda's contention always rested on the need for Vedic authority for image worship and not Purāṇic authority. He remained unconvinced that the Purāṇas were necessary for religious study.

Swami Dayananda's views on matters of scripture and worship aroused considerable interest so he decided to prepare the minds of his listeners to his chief objective and the views he held dear. The manifesto he prepared enumerated some of his beliefs with regard to religious practice. He believed that there were some practices that tended to debase and injure people religiously, and had to be avoided. Other practices elevated people spiritually because of their sublime truths.

The eight vices that he said debased people were:[9]

i. All works published by common man.
ii. The worship of stones in the belief that they represented *devatās*.
iii. The belief in the various sects.
iv. Vamamārgism as taught and practised in the Tantras.
v. The use of intoxicating drugs and liquor.
vi. Adultery.
vii. Fraud, conceit, lying, etc.
viii. Theft.

The virtues that he believed elevated people spiritually were: (Here quoted only in brief).

i. The twenty-one Śāśtras.
ii. Serving the guru and study of the Vedas.
iii. The performance of rituals like *sandhyā*, *agnihotra*.
iv. Conjugal faith and practice of moral discipline.
v. The practice of *tapas* (austerities) and self-control.
vi. Meditation and introspection; the cultivation of spiritual knowledge.
vii. A constant effort to observe rules of religious discipline and to avoid or conquer qualities such as lust, greed, anger and other vices.
viii. The practice of religious disciplines that would lead to *mokṣa*.

The manifesto resulted in large numbers of people taking a keen interest in the Swami and his work. Although Pandit Haldar was never able to quote the passages, in response to Dayananda's request he had a ready response. "If the Vedas do not enjoin idol worship where do they condemn it?" The Swami's reply was very lengthy but not convincing. Pandit Haldar did not give credence to his arguments and they parted company agreeing to disagree on a highly contentious matter.

THE ŚĀSTRĀRTHA AT BANARAS—1869

The Swami's first task on arrival in the city was to contact the leading *pundits* to arrange for a discussion on matters he considered important. Pandit Raja Ram Shastri was happy to arrange such a meeting and invited to it several other learned *pundits*. The Mahārājā of Kashi, on hearing of the proposed Śāstrārtha, agreed to direct proceedings. It was well publicised and drew a large crowd. As the city was known for its learning and the home of many learned *pundits*, the meeting was destined to prove one of the most important ever held by the Swami.[10]

The debates centred around several passages from the Vedas and other scriptures that Swami Dayananda found authoritative. The discussions were often interrupted by heckling and acrimony was very rife. The *Tattva-Bodhinī* of Calcutta had published in one of its weekly editions that none of the learned *pundits* was in a position to defeat the Swami in verbal battles.[11] He proved himself to be a formidable opponent, his most important concern being idolatry in its most debased form.

As in so many of the Swami's debates and disputations, there were heated arguments and as had happened so often they were vituperative and vitriolic in the extreme. The acrimony and animosities had engendered much unhappiness and the Swami had succeeded in making himself very unpopular among some people.

THE ŚĀSTRĀRTHA AT CHANDAPUR—1877

The Śāstrārtha at Chandapur was very significant because Swami Dayananda was joined in discussion by four Christian missionaries and two former Muslim scholars. The Swami's task in this discussion with representatives of these faiths was to assert Hindu viewpoints on matters of importance to the religious life of the people. The Śāstrārtha was intended to prove that with the Truth of the Vedas being a shining example to man of His glory, there was no need for such practices as conversion of people from one faith to another, but a need for harmony between peoples and greater respect for different religions. "And to achieve this it was necessary for Maulvis, Missionaries and ourselves to meet in love and peace and investigate the Truth."[12]

The two-day discussion was very extensive, with all parties

proffering many arguments and counter arguments in support of and in answer to contentious viewpoints. Swami Dayananda's contribution to the discussion was significant in that there were firstly the expected pleas for sober discussion whereby it would be possible to investigate Truth and determine which Faith was true. Secondly, he said, there was to be no harbouring of thoughts of victory and defeat as that was not the objective of the Śāstrārtha. Its sole purpose was to help all men investigate Truth that they may spiritually benefit by it. The Swami then proceeded to present the Hindu viewpoint on a wide variety of philosophical arguments concerning the nature of God and the world.

The discussion ended with all the parties still holding rigidly to their respective viewpoints but acknowledging that Swami Dayananda was a profound scholar of Vedic truth who had placed the participants under a debt of gratitude for sharing many valuable points of discussion with them.

DAYANANDA AND EDUCATION

Dayananda's Ideals in Education

Swami Dayananda's reflection on India's social condition led him to the conclusion that the educational system prevailing in the country was primarily responsible for her degradation. He therefore wanted to institute a new educational system which would incorporate totally revolutionary ideas to improve the prevailing social conditions. His first appeal went out to some of the prominent and wealthy citizens of Farrukhabad for assistance in the launching of a programme which would help to establish schools in many areas. His appeal received initial support from a few people sympathetic to his cause. The first such person was Lala Panna Lal Seth who had been building a *Śivālaya*.[13] He agreed to incorporate into this building a *pāṭhśālā* (a primary school), and to contribute to the salary of the first *pundit* employed to teach new religious ideas to the students.[14] Other friends came forward and offered money and other assistance to defray expenses for running of the school. The Swami himself a learned Sanskrit scholar, undertook to teach the *vidyārthīs* (young students) and to many he gave the *Yajñopavīta*, the sacred thread by which they were accepted into religious life.

Swami Dayananda knew no English, so his own education was completely indigenous, uninfluenced in any way by the system of education introduced by the British government.[15] He drew his information concerning the system of education to be introduced in India by the Arya Samaj wholly from Sanskrit sources. His beliefs thus suffered no indoctrination and his fierce and often vitriolic onslaughts against any such intrusion, particularly those advocated by people such as Charles Grant and other missionaries who pleaded for government assistance for Christian indoctrination, were as vociferous as they were tormented. The missionaries themselves were acutely aware that India's social conditions were due largely to the ignorance Indians displayed of their need for a proper understanding of religious and cultural ideals. Hindu inadequacy in formulating principles of education based on a sound system of educational philosophy made her vulnerable to the belief in the superiority of western educational systems. The new ideas thus imparted to Indians by British missionaries gave rise to the belief among Indians that Indian religious, cultural and educational standards were inferior.

Swami Dayananda recognised early in his career that many notions held by the Indian people about their religious, cultural and educational standards were very shortsighted.[16] He therefore emphasized the need for a totally new educational system and spared no effort in his attempt to establish this as part of his ideal of a total religious and cultural regeneration of the Indian people. In all his travels, wanderings and discussions among the people of north India he pleaded for the establishment of Sanskrit schools and the teaching of the Vedas as part of the curriculum.[17]

In his work *Satyartha Prakash*, Swami Dayananda lists fifty-one articles of faith which summarise his multifarious beliefs in the goodness of man when exposed to Vedic Truth. At a conference in Lahore in 1877 these fifty-one principles were reduced to ten basic teachings. The eighth of these principles reads: One should promote *Vidyā* and dispel *Avidyā*.

The Arya Samaj bases its stand on the principle that the dissemination of knowledge and the removal of ignorance are fundamental to its cause. In order to put into effect the educational ideas advocated by Swami Dayananda, two great educational institutions came into existence to conform to the programme then formulated. The first was the Dayanand Anglo-Vedic College, the very first branch of which was started at Lahore in 1886 under the direction of Lala Hans Raj. The second was the Gurukul, started under the direction of Swami Shraddhananda. The first Gurukul was established at Kangri.[18] Each of these institutions had its own educational objectives which were pursued with unrelenting vigour, often in the face of many challenges aroused by Muslim and Christian hostility. Swami Shraddhananda himself was assassinated by a Muslim fanatic in 1926.

The Arya Samaj has always been aware of the importance placed by Swami Dayananda on educational objectives for young people. The decision to establish the Dayanand Anglo-Vedic Colleges (often referred to as D.A.V. Colleges) was taken after his death to commemorate his work. The necessary funds came from various sources and a committee of interested people brought this institution into existence. The name of Lala Hans Raj was closely associated with the institution and its success was due to his guidance and direction as a leading educationist of his time. Lahore is now in Pakistan, so at the time of partition the Arya Samaj movement suffered grieviously from the loss of the first D.A.V. College that had been established there. The school was started as a secondary school but was later converted into a college, making it possible for students to study there for a B.A. degree. The D.A.V. College proved to be a very successful educational institution. The most important subjects taught were Sanskrit, Hindi, English, Persian, Philosophy, Ancient and Modern History, Political Economy, Logic, Elementary Physics and Chemistry.[19] The number of students that passed examinations was very large and those winning prizes for exemplary work were often conspicuous as students of D.A.V. Colleges. The movement thus developed a proud reputation for educational achievements. Several D.A.V. institutions were started in Punjab, Gujarat, Uttar Pradesh and elsewhere. Their total self-reliance, meaning that no assistance was received from Government or foreign sources, helped to establish great confidence in the institution. The Arya Samaj felt singularly proud of its achievement in the field of education as a result of the growth and development of these colleges.[20]

THE GURUKULA MOVEMENT

Swami Dayananda's ideal in education centred mainly on the study of Vedic culture through Sanskrit. The emphasis in the D.A.V. Colleges was laid on western values, hence a considerable deviation from Vedic values was discerned. In time, a number of criticisms were levelled against the educational ideal developing in D.A.V. Colleges. Among these were their pre-occupation with high levels of attainment at the expense of several of the more urgent needs of educational practices in the national interest. Inevitably, two rather distinct patterns of education appeared to develop when the established colleges became secular in their interests while several administrators appealed for religious interests to be served with greater zeal.

It thus became possible for the Arya Samaj to consider the establishment of what later emerged as the most original innovation in education in India: the Gurukula.[21] For many Indians the establishment of the Gurukula was an exciting prospect which led people like Rabindranath Tagore and others to see in it a resumption of ancient values and ideals that returned the country to her love for the recognition of her indigenous spirit and national feeling.

The primary aim of the Gurukula system was to acquaint students with Indian cultural life styles. Although western educational standards formed a focal point of interest, they were in effect secondary in importance.[22] It was hoped that the students of the Gurukula system could be moulded to develop love for everything noble in Indian culture. The teaching of Sanskrit and Hindi received considerable attention. Although most other. subjects had to be studied, it was expected that Indian culture would receive primary attention. In this way it was hoped that students would support the idea of home rule by never supporting the government, which at the time was British, thus asking students to agitate for independence and at the same time inculcating in them a love for educational programmes by which India's national interests could be emphasized through the teaching of, inter alia, agriculture and medical services.[23]

The Gurukula at Kangri developed considerably over a period of twenty years, from a small thatch-roofed building to a very large one incorporating several departments of school life. Students who graduated from the Gurukula were referred to as *Snātakas* and had titles such as Vedālaṅkār and Vidyālaṅkār conferred on them. The Kangri Gurukula, because of its location far away from the city centre, was a boarding school and no day scholars were allowed to attend it. The students were expected to study Sanskrit and Hindu religious literature, together with most other subjects. The entire course proved very popular with students, and a high standard of all-round achievement was maintained for many years. Apart from the regular schedule of activities that the boys observed each day it was expected that they would also perform the *Sandhyā* and *Agnihotra* ceremonies. The success of this system of education was not as widespread as that of the D.A.V. College, because they were primarily established in non-urban areas to cater to the rural requirements of the country.

For Swami Dayananda the massive regeneration of the country by revolutionary educational systems and standards was very important. In his *Satyartha Prakash* he elaborates on the numerous ideas he believed were necessary to be introduced into his new school systems.[24]

He regarded the following six principles as necessary for the implementation of a morally uplifting educational system:[25]

1. An educational edifice could only be built on sound religious and moral training.
2. He insisted on chastity and celibacy as the basis of physical culture.
3. Personal hygiene.
4. Student-teacher relationship should be close and, as far as possible, verging close to a father-son relationship.
5. Hindi should always be the medium of instruction.
6. A total eradication of the caste system, communal differences, class distinction and every other form of social prejudice.

Swami Dayananda was not opposed to the study of the English language and literature as such but he opposed the English educational system that was introduced into India, as this diverted people's attention from a love of Hindu culture.

The schools or pāṭhśālās he established had many strict rules, especially if they were boarding schools. Students had to observe rules of hygiene, diet, exercise, times of rising and sleeping and other forms of discipline. He took serious exception to any violation of rules by both teachers and students. It is now generally accepted that although Swami Dayananda himself was a man of great integrity and above all a man of great ideals, he never obtained the same level of co-operation and adherence to rules from others. Many of his assistants, both teachers and others, failed to follow the codes he laid down and the schools themselves were compelled to close down during his lifetime for want of greater commitment to his ideals.[26] However, when they were reopened by many of the stalwarts of the Arya Sámaj movement they proved in many ways to be an outstanding success, with many of India's foremost educationists expressing pride in the achievement of the Gurukulas. They were responsible for many outstanding contributions to formulating the highest objectives in educational aims and the methods of achieving them. These were based on high principles of education from which emerged a new educational philosophy. For students there was a new spirit of commitment to high discipline and character building which was aimed at developing a new national consciousness which kept religious values, historical tradition, concepts of working and ritual clearly in focus while yet not losing sight of developing trends in a modern, fast moving world of high technological advancement.

DAYANANDA'S WRITINGS

Swami Dayananda wrote many books in both Sanskrit and Hindi. V. Shastri lists about nineteen books, with *Satyartha Prakash*—The Light of Truth—as the greatest.[27]

SATYARTHA PRAKASH

This is a comprehensive work covering a wide range of moral and religious beliefs. It is written in two parts, the first of which comprises ten chapters and the second four chapters. The author summarises the entire work in what are referred to as the fifty-one articles of faith.

THE ṚG VEDA BHĀŚYA BHŪMIKĀ[28]

The *Rigvedadi Bhāśya Bhūmikā*, as it is better known, is a Sanskrit-Hindi work which forms an introduction to the Ṛg Veda Bhāśya.

THE PAÑCH-MAHĀYAJÑA-VIDHĪ

This little work deals with the five great daily duties of every householder, which Dayananda lists as:

Brahma Yajña: which advocates meditation on God twice a day.

Deva Yajña: a sacrifice called homa or agnihotra for the creation of a peaceful atmosphere of prayer and peace.

Pitṛa Yajña: which advocates ministry to the wise and learned.

Balivaiśva Yajña: feeding the poor.

Atithī Yajña: for discharging hospitality to friends known and unknown.

THE SAṀSKĀRAVIDHĪ

This is a treatise on ritual ceremonies and deals with the performance of the principal ceremonies associated with the life of a person from birth until death.

THE FOUNDING OF THE ARYA SAMAJ

Swami Dayananda formed the Arya Samaj in Bombay on 10 April 1875.[28] The formation of the Samaj had been one of the primary objectives of his life and preparation for it had been going on for many years. His association with a group of close friends who felt deeply committed to the ideals he set forth had made it possible for the Samaj to be formed with the aim of raising people from the depths of degradation to which Hindu society had been reduced.[29]

The words Arya and Samaj may be translated as "Association of Noble or Righteous People". The word Ārya makes no reference to any particular race, religion, sect or caste and aims only at character development. Thus the Arya Samaj is known as the "Society of Righteous Persons". That the members are expected to live by high moral principles is a tenet of the faith.

To this movement fell the task of protecting and propagating the scientific, theological basis of Vedic religion as expounded by Dayananda. His contention was "The Arya Samaj is a religious movement not merely in the sense that it is concerned with worship, prayer and philosophy, but its teachings embrace every aspect of life."

In all of Swami Dayananda's teachings, he stressed *ad nauseam* that the Vedas were the central authority for all religious Truth and that mankind had to follow this truth alone and no other. Thus he said and repeated time and again, that his sole mission in life was to preach, not a new religion or a new creed, but the ancient faith of Āryāvarta, preached by all the great teachers of Hinduism. This truth, he said, was the message of the Vedas, the eternal truth revealed by God to man at the beginning of time and intended to last until the end of time when all mankind had come to know it in all its fullness and glory.

It thus stands to reason that the constitution of the Arya Samaj had to bear a clause which stated clearly that the Vedas and the Vedas alone, had to form the absolute, authoritative basis for all matters affecting the religious life of Hindus everywhere. This in effect meant that while the Arya Samaj preached no dogma as such, it had to concede however that the declaration on the authority and infallibility of the Vedas was a dogma forming the basis of the Arya Samaj movement. Swami Dayananda also regarded several subsidiary scriptures as important. These were the six Vedāṅgas, the four Upavedas and the six Darśanas.

Some twenty-eight clauses formed the creed of the Samaj. These were read to the meeting on its opening day and accepted as its basic principles. The foundation of the Samaj had necessarily to be based on several guiding principles of religious conception in the light of the corruption that the Swami encountered in his travels around the country.

However, at a subsequent congress held in Lahore in 1877 the twenty-eight principles were reduced to ten and these now form the ten important guiding principles of the Samaj, accepted by all Arya Samajists more as guiding commandments. Every Samajist is expected to subscribe to these. They are more strictly in the nature of moral precepts which seek to guide the adherent to a high moral and ethical standard. Thus all who join the movement have no objection to accepting them. One of the principles makes reference to the monotheistic nature of the faith of the Samaj and another that the Vedas are the repository of the true knowledge of God. It is therefore the paramount duty of every Arya Samajist to learn them and teach them to others. The following are the ten principles of the Arya Samaj[30]:

1. God is the primary source of all true knowledge and all that is known by its means.
2. God is existent, intelligent and blissful. He is formless, omniscient, just, merciful, unborn, endless, unchangeable, beginningless, the support of all, the master of all, omnipresent, immanent, unaging, immortal, fearless, eternal and holy and the maker of all. He alone is worthy of being worshipped.
3. The Vedas are the scriptures of true knowledge. It is the first duty of the Āryans to read them, teach them, recite them and hear them being read.
4. One should always be ready to accept truth and give up untruth.

5. One should do everything according to the dictates of *Karma* after consideration of right and wrong.
6. Doing good to the whole world is the primary objective of this Society, i.e. to ameliorate the physical, spiritual and social conditions of all men.
7. All people should be treated with care, justice, righteousness and due regard to their merits.
8. Ignorance ought to be dispelled and knowledge disseminated.
9. One should not be content with one's own welfare alone, but should look to the welfare of all.
10. In all matters affecting the well-being of society, one should subordinate personal interests; in matters that affect him alone, he is to enjoy freedom of action.

Swami Dayananda himself never became a member of the Arya Samaj. He had vowed never to introduce a 'guru cult' into it because he had been made aware of the evils of this form of religious exploitation. For this reason he became adamant in his teaching that all men were born equal and that the Samaj had to build its doctrinal edifice on the principles of equality, with no distinction being made regarding caste, position, learning, sex or economic standing.

The primary aim of the Arya Samaj was to do good to mankind, i.e. to ameliorate the physical, spiritual and social conditions of all men. The Swami, however, was primarily concerned about the Hindu community and improving conditions in order to eliminate the degraded standards of behaviour to which society had been reduced. He made it obligatory for the members to embrace truth and reject falsehood. In becoming members of the Arya Samaj they were expected never to feel gratified in their own betterment, but always to work for the welfare of others. This welfare incorporated their physical, material and spiritual well-being. He chose not to elaborate on theoretical doctrines. That was why he reduced the number of principles of the Samaj to ten and tried to present the code of ethical behaviour and moral obligations as succinctly as possible.[31]

The Arya Samaj thus basically and essentially is a body of noble people believing in the divine authority of the Vedas as revealed by God to man for the purpose of declaring his love for mankind. Swami Dayananda thus asserted that the religion he preached was not new. It was the eternal truth taught in the Vedas and reinterpreted time and again by many of the great sages of India. Swami Dayananda was vehemently opposed to the corruption of the pure Āryan faith and the influence of Christianity and Islam upon his people. His call was for his people to go back to the Vedas and to assert themselves as upholders of the truest and most ancient of faiths. Whilst he was wary of the attacks made against Hinduism by Christians and Muslims, he was more interested in purging Hinduism of its many superstitions, prejudices and idolatrous observances. His own spiritual ideas were born of the experiences he underwent throughout his life. He was thus dedicated to preaching the gospel from a radically different angle in the hope that a new and lasting code of religious commitment could be introduced into the ancient land of Āryāvrata, his native land and the home of the ancient faith he so deeply loved and cherished.

REFERENCES

1. Farquhar, J.N., *Modern Religious Movements in India*, Munshiram Manoharlal, Delhi, 1977.
2. Singh, B.C., *Ibid*, p. 42.
3. Sarda, H.B., *Ibid*, p. 24.
4. Sarda, H.B., *Ibid*, p. 36.
5. Rolland, R., *Ibid*, p. 131.
6. Singh, B.C., *Ibid*, p. 46.
7. Satyaprakash, S., *Ibid*, p. 16.
8. Singh, B.C., *Ibid*, p. 47.
9. Lillington, Frank, *The Brahmo Samaj*.
10. Sastri, V., *Ibid*, p. 16.
11. Sarda, H.B., *Ibid*, p. 41.
12. Aurobindo, S., *Ibid*, p. 13.
13. Sastri, V., *Ibid*, p. 16.
14. Pareek, R.S., *Contribution of Arya Samaj in the Making of Modern India*, Rajasthan University, Jaipur, 1965, p. 80.
15. Pareek, R.S., *Ibid*, p. 82.
16. Sarma, D.S., *Hinduism Through the Ages*, Bhavans, Bombay, 1956, p. 139.
17. Sarma, D.S., *Ibid*, p. 140.
18. Pandit, K.S., *A Critical Study of Arya Samaj Education*, Baroda University, Baroda, 1974, p. 54.
19. Pandit, K.S., *Ibid*, p. 205.
20. Pandit, K.S., *Ibid*, p. 207.
21. Pareek, R.S., *Ibid*, p. 86.
22. Pandit, K.S., *Ibid*, pp. 240-247.
23. Pandit, K.S., *Ibid*, p. 206.
24. Shastri, V., *Ibid*, p. 16
25. Singh, B.C., *Ibid*, p. 142.
26. Dayananda, S., *Satyartha Prakash*, Jan Gyan Prakashan, Delhi, 1978.
27. Padale, P.D., *The Endowed Arya Samaj*.
28. Shastri, V., *Ibid*.
29. Upadhyaya, G.P., *Reason and Religion*.
30. Pareek, R.S., *Ibid*, p. 49.
31. Pareek, R.S., *Ibid*.

CHAPTER 3

Muslim and Christian Influences

INDIA HAS always been regarded as an integral part of Asia. Various people have come to her territory, mostly in search of her legendary treasures. While many were passing adventurers, some made India their permanent home and stayed here to become a fateful part of her history and culture.[1] Unlike the far eastern influences of the Chinese and the Japanese that were rich and ancient, Roman and Greek influences were slight, while Persian and other Āryan influences of an earlier era were more substantial. The first of the Muslims to visit India, in the eighth century A.D., were the Arabs, who were temporary sojourners. They were followed three centuries later by the Turks, who established themselves there permanently.[2]

Muhamed Babur, the Muslim Moghul ruler, said it was always in his heart to possess Hindustan either peacefully or by force.[3] In 1000 A.D. and the years following, Mohamed of Gazni led no fewer than seventeen expeditions which laid the foundations of a powerful Muslim empire in India. India was ruled for more than six centuries by Moghul rulers until the coming of the European traders and their free grab of power in a powerless, leaderless Hindu sub-continent.

European influence began with Vasco da Gama and the Portuguese in 1498.[4] They were followed by the Dutch, the French and the British. The company of merchants in London trading as the British East India Company, having received their charter from Queen Elizabeth, soon established trade links that filled the sea lanes of India with traffic heavily laden with spices and other riches of the East. Other Englishmen set foot on Indian soil to spread the message of the Christian gospel, while nebulous and negligent Hindu saints wandered from village to village oblivious of the wealth foreigners usurped with unbridled callousness.

In the centuries that followed, Muslim and Christian missionaries and military efforts succeeded with aplomb.[5] The chief reason for this lay without doubt with Indians themselves. Riddled as it was with caste and communal prejudices and above all with an incorrigible lack of religious cohesiveness, Indian society found it difficult to formulate a singularly well-reasoned sense of socio-religious direction despite many centuries of deep-rooted interest in religion. Thus her floating mass of beliefs, customs, social practices and sometimes even grotesque ritualistic ideas formed the backdrop against which Hindus themselves had to search out with extreme difficulty a binding doctrinal base for a coherent Hindu unity. The two foreign faiths spread throughout the land, particularly in areas where poverty and caste prejudices ran deep and promises of freedom from their social and even economic shackles were heard with gullible impunity.

The growth and development of these two foreign faiths changed the face of Hindu India.[6] For many centuries they spread their influences while powerless Hindus paid dearly the price of religious naivete. Despite the grandeur of their faith and haughty claims of pride in it their pre-occupation with religious tolerance and respect for all religions exposed them to socio-cultural weaknesses that were the very bane of a society growing sterile with centuries of unchecked neglect and demeaning weaknesses of every kind.[7]

Hindu, Muslim and Christian animosities have simmered in India for many centuries.[8] Many people within the Arya Samaj movement have long felt deeply grieved that a Hindu nation could suffer such humiliation through millions of Indians being converted to foreign faiths, either forcibly or by seduction. It has always been obvious to all who are familiar with the situation that most converts are drawn from India's "lowest" castes. Her converts are rarely won by theological coercion but because of degraded social conditions in her poverty-stricken environment.[9] Hindu-Muslim friction is always characterised by violence while Hindu-Christian relations are plagued by seething verbal animosities. For instance, in 1897 Pandit Lekh Ram, an indefatigable worker for the Arya Samaj cause and a great stalwart and patriot in the movement,[10] was murdered by a Muslim. In 1903, Christian missionaries took advantage of famine relief operations to make converts.[11] In 1922 and 1923, during the reconversion from Islam of more than two thousand families who had been forcibly converted to Islam by the Moplah rebels in Malabar and the reconversion of more than 30,000 Malkana Rajputs in the villages of Rajputana, Arya Samajists worked strenously in the face of very great difficulties to avert massive apostasy.[12] The beginning of the Second World War in Europe coincided with growing hostilities between Hindus and Muslims in India which culminated in the partition of the country and the birth of a new country—Pakistan. This was seen by many as the ultimate irreparable humiliation Hindu India had to suffer in a situation engendered by British encouragement of religious intransigence.

India's political difficulties during the country's struggle for independence heightened religious friction, especially between Hindus and Muslims. Muslim vociferousness has always been pronounced and despite their being a minority group in India their force as a religious community has been extraordinarily powerful. Both Christian and Muslim proselytizing in this economically backward country has for centuries been very successful. Murray Titus observes that, "throughout the whole period of Muslim contact with India, the attitude of Muslim rulers to their Hindu subjects and their religion has been very largely one of intolerance or indifference."[13] Very much the same can be said of Christian attitudes towards indigenous Hinduism. The struggle of Hindus and Hinduism against invading intolerance has therefore been the backbone of her struggle for socio-political survival with the plea for unity and strength the watchwords of hope even at the present time.

In his work *Satyartha Prakash*, Swami Dayananda is unsparing in his criticism of Islam and Christianity. Apart from the mere fact of the intrusion of these two foreign faiths into India, their criticism and total lack of appreciation of many of the finer points of Hinduism were, he felt, grossly unjust and disrespectful.[14] He chose, therefore, during the course of his teachings and ministry "to pay back these two aggressors in their own coin."[15] The Arya Samaj movement was sometimes described therefore as a movement of self-defence. It is for this reason that the Arya Samaj has often carried on a vigorous campaign of propaganda against Islam and Christianity and thus to reconvert as many Hindus as possible who were drawn into these faiths through ignorance and short-sightedness. The Samaj carried on a militant campaign to reintroduce a tone of manliness into its beliefs which it had lost as a result of centuries of Moghul, and later British rule. Muslim agitation against *Satyartha Prakash*, particularly its fourteenth chapter, resulted in a Government rule being enforced to restrict its distribution.[16] The Arya Samaj had its stronghold in Lahore, now in Pakistan, the birth of which resulted in the movement losing millions of rupees worth of property and untold millions of selfless workers in the ensuing conflagration of partition.

Swami Dayananda's well-known method of dialogue through the

holding of Śāstrārthas was continued by members of the Arya Samaj movement and proved popular for many years. These Śāstrārthas were instrumental in helping Arya Samaj workers to convince converts and would-be converts that Hinduism had much to offer; also the Vedic faith was eulogised to thwart possible conversion of hundreds of people.

Swami Dayananda's argument against the presence in India of foreign faiths stems largely from the distrust he had for their preachers and more especially for the methods they used in proselytizing their message. Conversion through the use of force has been characteristic of Islam since the days of Jehangir and his ready willingness to express his belief in *Jizya*.

> "Fight those who believe not
> In God nor the Last Day...
> ...(even if they are)
> Of the People of the Book
> Until they pay the Jizya
> With willing submission
> And feel themselves subdued."[17]

And again:

> "Fight for the religion of God against those who fight against you. And kill them wherever you find them; for temptation to idolatry is more grievous than slaughter."[18]

Using these quotations from the Korān, Muslim invaders sought to usurp through rape and pillage all that lay before them. And in the six centuries since the first Muslims set foot on Indian soil the carnage was continued even after the split of the land and the birth of Pakistan.

Hindu-Christian animosities, quite unlike Hindu-Muslim antagonism, were largely verbal duels that engendered much hatred. For many centuries, however, these animosities have simmered and, unlike the characteristic stand of peace and harmony that Hinduism has always preached, as epitomised in the work of Mahatma Gandhi, Christian missionaries have always fanned the flames of hatred by antagonising Hindus through coercive propaganda aimed at winning new converts.[19]

Among the many meetings that Swami Dayananda held to discuss matters of scriptural importance, the Śāstrārtha held at Chandapur in March 1877 was one of the most significant, as it was held among representatives of the three faiths.[20] Swami Dayananda and Munshi Indramani represented Hinduism. The Christians were the Rev. T.G. Scott; Rev. Noble; Rev. Parker; and Rev. Thompson. Islam was represented by Maulvi Mohamed Quasim and Sayyed Abul Mansoor. In the two days in which discussions were held Muslim and Christian feelings ran high and discussions were replete with innuendos of every kind. Swami Dayananda's view reflected an age-old Hindu stand in which he exhorted men to understand each other. He said, "To me it seems best that the Moulvis, the Missionaries and ourselves should meet in love and peace and investigate the Truth. No one should be hostile to others."[21] These opening remarks set the tone for the two-day meeting which culminated in the men believing that there was much to be gained through dialogue and that the age-old methods employed by Christian and Muslim missionaries could do with much reconsideration.

The outstanding contribution made by Swami Dayananda to religious understanding in India was his exhortation to all people, irrespective of caste or religious affiliation, to strive to be Āryas, noble people whose characters rather than family background would reflect their religious standing in every walk of life.[22] This, he said, was the concept of Āryans as people which transcends the communal barriers that have plagued Indian history for many centuries.[23] The intrusion of two foreign faiths, in Dayananda's view, was the addition of two new movements that further divided a nation heavily burdened by massive dissension and strife. He saw Islam and Christianity as destroyers of her basic structure in ways he found difficult to comprehend as so many of the practices of engendering religious animosities they indulged in were totally contrary to everything he understood in terms of true religious practice.

Swami Dayananda's incessant call was for Hindus to return to the teachings of the Vedas.[24] He saw his own message as irrevocably intertwined with the call for a return to the essentials of the faith. This eliminates any extraneous beliefs such as idolatry which in turn introduce sterile and some unacceptable practices into the whole religious edifice he conceived. If the call then was for Hindus to "return to the Vedas", it became inevitable that antagonism towards foreign faiths and more particularly irreligious practices within Hinduism should grow. Swami Dayananda preached a movement of reform on nationalistic and indigenous lines. And many of the religious practices he advocated he hoped would flourish with the same fervour evinced by Muslim and Christian adherents to their respective faiths.

Swami Dayananda was deeply indebted to both Islam and Christianity in two respects, which he readily introduced into the Arya Samaj movement.[25] He saw firstly that the Christian practice of congregational worship led by a preacher of good standing was of primary importance to systematic worship. He regarded this as one of the cornerstones of his rejuvenation policy which had virtually no parallel in the Hinduism of his time. His "back to the Vedas" call was, however, a reminder to many that congregations and systematic, organised, congregational worship was not unknown in Vedic times. The *yajña* was performed only if a small group of people gathered together and Dayananda's call encouraged congregations to gather for worship.

From the Muslim people in India Swami Dayananda learnt what it meant for masses of people to adhere to a faith with fanatical zeal.[26] He often repeated that if Hindus could awake to the same fighting spirit as the Muslims and not "sleep like Kumbhakarna", Hinduism would awake to a new dawn.[27] The basis of the call was his zealous condemnation of mythological, ritual-ridden Purāṇic Hinduism, and a return to the main tenets of Sanātana Dharma that imbibed purified conceptions of God, man and the divine relationship by which they were united.

The Arya Samaj has since its formation been epitomised by a great amount of virility and combativeness which have long been a trait absent in the religion practised by Hindus throughout the country in all ages of her history. Swami Dayananda was happy to see some of the enthusiasm that existed within many Christian organisations fill the Arya Samaj movement, which within a short period spread to many parts of the country. Its import to other countries, including South Africa, was the direct result of the tone of virility he imparted into it on the model of the Christian and Muslim movements that spread their gospels with such ease in his God-fearing country. Thus many of the practices that form an important part of the Arya Samaj services are now mirrored in the lessons learnt from traditional Christian services. He also extolled the spirit of enthusiasm in Islam which allows for a turning to prayer no less than five times a day. The Arya Samaj does, however, invite some anxiety among students of

Hindu movements who see the movement developing into a sect, because *Satyartha Prakash* has virtually become its canonised holy scripture.

South African Arya Samaj now finds its roots being implanted in the same spirit which engenders belief among Muslims that Islam is the greatest religion in the world, while Christians exclaim exclusive salvation through one great Saviour. It is now clear that the strength and virility evinced by the movement in this country emanate from the strength, vigour, and above all, the sincere convictions of the man Arya Samajists so greatly admire.

REFERENCES

1. Smith, Vincent, A., *The Oxford History of India, ed.* Perceval Spear, Oxford, Delhi, 1958.
2. Sharma, S.R., *The Making of Modern India,* Orient Longmans, Bombay, 1951.
3. Smith, V.A., *Ibid.*
4. Sharma, S.R., *Ibid.*
5. Smith, V.A., *Ibid.*
6. Titus, Murray, T., *Indian Islam*, Oriental Books Corp., Delhi, 1979.
7. Kraemer, H., *World Cultures and World Religions,* Latterworth Press, London, 1960.
8. Wolpert, S., *A New History of India*, Oxford University Press, New York, 1977.
9. Titus, M.T., *Ibid.*
10. Demodaran, T., *Indian Thought: A Critical Survey*, Asia Publishing House, Bombay, 1867.
11. Sarma, D.S., *Hinduism Through the Ages*, Bhavans, Bombay, 1956.
12. Sarma, D.S., *Ibid.*
13. Sarma, D.S., *Ibid.*
14. Titus, M.T., *Indian Islam*, Orient Books Corporation, Delhi, 1979.
15. Farquhar, J.N., *Modern Religious Movements in India*, Munshiram Manoharlal, Delhi, 1977.
16. Sarma, D.S., *Ibid.*
17. Holy Koran, *Sura IX*, 29, Tr. Abdullah Yusuf Alli.
18. Holy Koran, *Ibid.*
19. Ranganathananda, S., *Eternal Values for a Changing Society*, Bharatiya Vidya Bhavan, Bombay, 1971.
20. Singh, B.C., *Life and Teachings of Swami Dayananda*, Jan Gyan Prakashan, New Delhi, 1971.
21. Singh, B.C., *Ibid.*
22. Sarda, H.B., *Life of Dayananda Saraswati,* Vedic Yantralaya, Ajmer, 1946.
23. Singh, B.C., *Ibid.*
24. Sarma, D.S., *Ibid.*
25. Dayananda, S., *Satyartha Prakash*, Jan Gyan Prakashan, Delhi, 1977.
26. Karaemer, H., *Ibid.*
27. Sarda, H.B., *Ibid.*

SECTION THREE

ARYA SAMAJ IN SOUTH AFRICA

Introduction

BEFORE ENTERING into a discussion on the Arya Samaj as a religious movement making a strong impact on the socio-cultural values held by some Hindus in South Africa, we need to consider the frame of reference against which we plan to consider the structural-functional implications of its existence and impact.

The reformation that Swami Dayananda initiated in Hindu society was welcomed by a large section of people who appreciated its reformative motives. More than anything else his call was for people to reconsider the purpose and function of scripture as the repository of what he termed the message of eternal truth. Truth cut across all the other popular notions held by Hindus for centuries about the myths and rituals and the religious practices that dominated Indian life for many centuries. Swami Dayananda held strong views on the caste system, child marriage, untouchability, widow remarriage, reconversion of Hindus to Hinduism and several other aspects of Indian life. His strong convictions on these and other matters led to a search for, and discovery of, a new religious system with totally new approaches to religious practice. The Arya Samaj was formed to bring into existence a new order of soundness and vitality to an Indian society burdened with superstition and degenerative weaknesses of every kind.

Our task here is to consider the superordinate meaningfulness of the objectives of the Arya Samaj and to attempt an analysis of the reason why such a movement may lay claim to the role of a religious action system with a strong structural-functional base of operation.

The first consideration will be the structural category concerning the acceptance of the authority of the Vedas as revealed truth and the resulting theological overtones that exemplify religious conception among Arya Samajists in particular and Hindus in general. The second will be the functional category of the reform in social practices such as, inter alia, the caste system and *Śuddhī*. And the third will be in the area of religious understanding. Neo-Hinduism now marks a considerable divergence from some age-old practices that have come to be recognised as unacceptable malpractices having no religious meaning.

It is not the writer's intention in this study to apply any hierarchical distinction to the components of the social actions emanating from the prescribed religious behaviour of Arya Samajists. What the writer intends, however, is to consider the recommendations of Smelser[1] by analysing the components of religious action in the light of the superordinate meaning system emanating from the understanding of religious practice *per se* on the part of Arya Samajists themselves.

Swami Dayananda's pronouncements have now become the verbal symbols par excellence within the empirical purview of the movement. These symbols, in a phenomenological sense, reveal the deepest aspects of reality for a young, deeply religious community. The symbols are a means of knowledge. Brede Kristensen[2] suggests that symbols indicate the essence of reality and such symbols are represented by the new approaches arising from the reformative principles advocated by Dayananda. The remarkable feat of the achievement lies in the maintenance of religious action that revolutionised the symbolic action which advocated far-reaching reforms, while yet maintaining the cultural enterprise that is distinctively Hindu. The human relationships that now mark out the Arya Samaj movement have come to epitomise new expressions of meanings and shared values in social life and also to initiate similar shared values in religious expression. Vernon[3] writes that symbols identify things or practices and provide plans of action. Dayananda's plan of action, in the South African sense, was to introduce new social meaning to age-old religious teachings.

REFERENCES

1. Smelser, J.N., *Theory of Collective Behaviour*, Routledge, Kegan and Paul, London, 1962.

2. Kristenson, B.W., *The Meaning of Religion*, Marinus Nyboth, The Hague, 1860, p. 410.

3. Vernon, J.M., *Sociology of Religion*, McGraw Hill, New York, 1962, p. 77.

CHAPTER 1

Historical Perspective

THE ARRIVAL OF Indians in South Africa under agreements of indenture, was the result of their search for economic prosperity in an environment that was always unfortunately politically hostile.[1] The socio-political difficulties the Indian people encountered on their arrival here were largely responsible for the growth of the state of religious limbo into which they had been plunged. Some time was required for adjustment to their new situation—a situation that never accommodated their traditional practices in the way they had been used to in their native land. The kind of religious infrastructure necessary for assisting them to accommodate a strange new environment was sadly lacking, and this brought with it a host of problems in addition to the crucial socio-political ones they faced in a hostile western country.

The seeds of religious ferment in the Hindu community thus began to germinate almost from the very moment of their arrival in Natal, with their agitation marked by an escalation in religious and even theological misunderstanding. For more than forty years, many persons of concern believed that a need for religious reform, more particularly as Swami Dayananda had conceived it, needed to be introduced into South African Hinduism. Contact with India heightened this feeling and soon a lead was taken to set in motion the machinery of innovation for drastic reform. The view that changes to modes of worship had to be made was supported by several leaders perceptive of the growing decay in religious standards. Modes of worship within the Hindu community varied from the most acutely ritualistic to the highly devotional, with the emphasis on familial themes that were seldom, if ever, based on scriptural injunctions supported by any form of theological exegesis.

Since these patterns of worship had had their origins in India, leading Arya Samajists concluded that the very seeds of destruction that Swami Dayananda had been familiar with there, had their corresponding similarities in South Africa.

From 1860 to the turn of the century, Hindus in South Africa were kept in a state of religious limbo. Although many Hindu temples were constructed during this period,[2] their main purpose was the observance of rituals such as they had been familiar with all their lives. There were no religious institutions that disseminated any religious literature and none of the temples was known to discourse a specific doctrine except those preached through ritual and sacrificial worship. Hence no theological foundations were laid and all religious education was conducted through a kinship structure peculiar to the joint family system which obtained in the community at the time.

Apart from the fact that "kinsmen" are regarded by South African Hindus as of primary importance for the purpose of deriving social value and status in the community, religious perversions were allowed to dominate if "more knowledgeable" elders dictated these religious terms. It became a customary practice in most Hindu homes of any language group for one person to attain a position of religious eminence or religious merit by deriving a special ability to perform rituals and ceremonies. In this way he or she was elevated to a position of authority and thereby was free to practise religion, even if only in its most ritualistic form.

Priests in the Hindu community in South Africa have never been known to graduate from theological colleges. All priests, from whatever language group they may come, inherit their profession by studying under the guidance of a Guru, whose qualifications invariably comprised a sound knowledge of some religious literature either in Sanskrit or some other Indian language, an ability to perform numerous ceremonies, marriage and death ceremonies being the most common, and perhaps also able to conduct a vernacular class wherever facilities for it became available. In many instances he was closely associated with a temple. By this is meant that he was a resident priest called on to perform the usual rituals that accompany every worship.

Pandit Nardev Vedalankar[3] believes that when the first followers of the Arya Samaj movement of India arrived in South Africa at the turn of the century "they were alarmed at the spiritual and religious degeneration of their Hindu brethren in this country". Hilda Kuper[4] similarly observes that, apart from the average Hindu being relatively ignorant, Hindu masses "act their religion and don't think it". The emphasis in the criticism was that the acts were so grotesque as to be totally devoid of any real religious meaning. Ritual and dogma often form the focal point of religious behaviour in every religion, but within Hinduism they exacerbate a form of religious degeneration with sometimes quite alarming results. Swami Dayananda was only too well aware of this in his long career as a religious reformer.

Enthusiastic sympathisers of the Arya Samaj cause saw numerous opportunities in South Africa for introducing reforms in religious concept and behaviour. An appeal was made to Pandit Hans Raj[5] and soon thereafter South Africa's Hindu community, or one small segment of it at any rate, awaited with enthusiasm the coming of one who was to set the scene for a new religious nativity in South Africa.

Visits to South Africa by prominent Indians were prompted largely by political considerations. Although Mahatma Gandhi's visit was initiated by a legal tangle involving a business firm,[6] he stayed to fashion an Indian political consciousness that could possibly have been foreseen before his arrival. Among the prominent religious leaders to visit the country the very first was Professor Bhai Parmanand.[7] His arrival on 5th August 1905 was well publicised and his tour of South Africa at a very crucial period in the history of the Indian people is remembered as a milestone for religious reform and regeneration. Despite the enormous political turmoil and the hazards that surrounded the relationship between Indians and Whites in Natal during these early years, Professor Bhai Parmanand's visit was a marked success. He was the first important Arya Samajist to visit this country; so his talks, lectures and visits to selected areas had a marked effect on general religious interest. His tour of Natal and the Transvaal lasted four months.

At the time of Professor Parmanand's visit, the Hindu Indian community was experiencing its most crucial political difficulties. Also Hindu religious immaturity appeared to have reached a new low in degeneration. Members of the Tamil community had no other recourse to religious affiliation apart from the ritual of Kavadi, while among Hindi-speaking people the familiar *Kathā* that few could understand, was popular.

The establishment of the Arya Samaj in India had strong implications for Arya Samaj activity in South Africa. The growth of interest in Swami Dayananda led to the establishment of small groups that ultimately grew to become formally constituted organisations although with purely local interest. One such group was the Ved Dharma Sabha of Pietermaritzburg, which was the forerunner of the national Arya Samaj movement in South Africa. Several other groups were started by people whose influence in the community did not extend beyond their local geographical limits. It was clear that with the kind of religious activity that was now becoming a part of the Hindu scene in Natal between 1900 and 1925, the stage was being set for the formation of an Arya Samaj movement of national importance.

Swami Dayananda's preaching tours of many North Indian towns and villages meant that after his decision to revert to speaking Hindi his influence spread rapidly among all Hindi speaking people of North India. It was inevitable, therefore, that his message in South Africa was confined largely to the Hindi-speaking community in this country. Because he was born a Gujarati, his influence among Gujarati-speaking people was strong, but nothing like the impact he had on the Hindi community of Natal.

Hilda Kuper observes: "A house in an Indian area is never an isolated dwelling; it is integrated into the street, neighbourhood and community. Kinsmen often live near each other, affairs of neighbours arouse the gossip that controls the moral standards of the whole area; temples and schools are subscribed by local donations and become local and public meeting places; shops give credit to the families in the area; the local community develops an in-group awareness expressed in a number of local institutions."[8] It was in this way that even the most influential of messages could be disseminated. Also, the more activist influence of political thinking that occupied the minds of so many Indians because of the oppressive political climate in which they lived, spread.

"An Englishman's home is his castle", says Hilda Kuper, and "an Indian's home is his shrine". In Hindu homes, Hinduism is the dominant idiom of South African Indian life, the hearth is sacred, ritual plants are grown in the yard, a special room or part of a room is used for regular family prayers."[9] If this was the setting for a family gathering for the purpose of prayer, it was also the setting for the birth and germination of the seeds of religious awareness that culminated in the establishment of organisations such as the Arya Samaj and others in South Africa.

Discussion on sources of religious differentiation leads to an examination of the outcomes derived from such differentiation. Group structures are seen to emanate within a formalised group pattern which follows in the development of different group structures. Group structures are based largely upon relationships between religion and society. An attempt is made in this section to analyse the causes of religious differentiation, and to relate the variations in religious structure to the question of the functions of religion.

Milton Yinger observes, "Most classification of religious groups start from the basic distinction, first fully developed by Ernst Troeltsch, between the church and the sect."[10] An interesting observation too concerns the methodological sophistication developing with reference primarily to the structure of a group affiliation, even if any form of guided leadership was absent. Our instrument of analysis assists in minimizing the similarities that mark out the religious organisations within the Hindu community which share a common socio-cultural system. The attempt to isolate the Arya Samaj is done to effect an analysis of a single religious innovation that is singularly divergent from all other institutions more particularly those serving the needs of a single minority and the typology constructs found within it.

The emphasis in the Arya Samaj is on sacrament and creeds and that of the Samajist himself on "right" or "noble" behaviour. The dual co-operation of action and ideal has resulted in an effort at social cohesion and order. The Samaj strives to be co-extensive with society to bring Hindus within its purview of nobility in religious action. Salvation for Samajists rests not only upon ethical achievement but also upon sacrament and acquiescence within its own creed to the norms it circumscribes. Thus religious discipline for Hindus as a whole, as the Arya Samaj conceives it, excludes those who question its premises, rather than those who fail to realise its growing noble standards.

This function of social reintegration and constructive religious engagement was conceived as ideal for Samajic work in South Africa. Its support for a new social order enabled it to create a growth of possibilities at the turn of the century which culminated in a historic achievement with the formation of an institution to express palpably its noble intention.

REFERENCES

1. Meer, F., *Portrait of Indian South Africans*, Avon House, Durban, 1969.
2. Nowbath, R.S., Choria S. et Lalla, *The Hindu Heritage in South Africa*, Hindu Maha Sabha, Durban, 1960.
3. Vedalankar, N., *Religious Awakening in South Africa*, Arya Pratinidhi Sabha, Natal, 1950, p. 15.
4. Kuper, H., *Indian People in Natal*, Natal University Press, Durban, 1960.

5. Vedalankar, N., *Ibid,* p. 15.
6. Gandhi, M.K., *An Autobiography*, Navjivan Publishing House, Ahmedabad, 1940.
7. Vedalankar, N., *Ibid,* p. 40.
8. Kuper, H., *Ibid,* p. XV.
9. Kuper, H., *Ibid.*
10. Yinger, M., *The Scientific Study of Religion*, McMillan Company, London, 1970, p. 251.

CHAPTER 2

Eminent Arya Samajists

SINCE THE arrival of the first Indians in South Africa in 1860, many eminent Hindu teachers paid visits here. Most came with the intention of propagating religious ideals in various forms, while others arrived for purely political reasons as official delegates representing the Indian Government. Although some of these teachers were people who were little known outside the Hindu community, others were people of international repute. One of them was "moulded" in this country to be recognised internationally as one of the great men of the twentieth century.[1] The task in this section will be primarily to assess the contribution made to the theological perspectives of the Arya Samaj movement in this country and to consider this contribution to the growth and development of Hindu thought nationally.

Pandit Nardev Vedalankar lists the names of seven Arya Samajists who visited South Africa in the years immediately following the formation of the Arya Samaj organisation.[2] He also lists the names of seven other important visitors to South Africa as teachers and students of Hinduism. Although not strictly speaking Arya Samajists, their respect for and acceptance of many Arya Samaj principles qualified them for inclusion in his book.[3] A third category of persons listed by Pandit Nardev is the group of South African Indians which preached Arya Samaj ideals in this country at various times in its history.

It is necessary to note at this stage that South Africa's Hindu community comprises people of four language groups: viz. Hindi, Tamil, Telegu and Gujarati. Although people from each of these language communities have taken a deep interest in the Arya Samaj movement, its impact was always felt among Gujarati and above all Hindi people.

The birth of the Arya Samaj movement in India was felt with growing interest world wide. The spread of the movement among the people of Uttar Pradesh and Bihar in India meant that friends and relatives of people in these states who had emigrated to countries like Fiji,[4] Mauritius, East Africa, Surinam, Trinidad and Guyana would express great sympathy and support for the Arya Samaj movement. It was inevitable that South African supporters would extend invitations to prominent Arya Samajists to visit this country. That Professor Bhai Parmanand was the first Hindu teacher of merit ever to visit this country is significant because he was invited by supporters of the movement in this country.

Professor Parmanand arrived on 5th August 1905.[5] It is significant that no Arya Samaj movement was going to result from the professor's visit because, as Pandit Nardev Vedalankar observes: "On account of religious and linguistic differences, the formation of an Arya Samaj was not feasible."[6] The professor's visit had therefore necessarily been confined to many talks and some preaching in various towns in Natal.[7]

Professor Parmanand's visit is not remembered by anyone today. But records indicate that it had enormously far-reaching consequences, firstly for Hinduism generally and secondly for the Arya Samaj movement in particular.[8] The professor, a faculty member at Lahore College, became familiar to his associates in this country as "Bhaiji" when he toured major centres in Natal and the Transvaal. He was an eloquent speaker who moved people with evangelical force and conviction to rethink their waning interest in Hindu teachings. Mahatma Gandhi, who was in Johannesburg at the time, was elected Chairman of the Reception Committee. The tour the professor undertook was significant because it had an effect on many Hindus and afforded them their first ever opportunity of listening to a Hindu evangelist preaching the word of God in a new strain. The professor spoke mainly in Hindi but was readily able to express himself in English as well. This was necessary as many of his listeners were non-Hindi speaking people.

The professor stayed in South Africa for just over four months. The time was used for preaching a spiritual and cultural message but it was totally inadequate for stimulating the formation of any institution of either provincial or national significance. However, the Hindu Young Men's Association became known throughout Natal and its adherence to the study of Vedic literature had wide repercussions for the community as a whole.

Sri Swami Shankaranandaji Maharaj arrived in South Africa on 4th October 1908.[9] Described as "an ambassador for Hinduism", he proved to be a worthy missionary who preached not only Arya Samaj principles but the message of Hinduism in its broadest form.

The Swami's perceptiveness led to his gentle attack against much of the superstition, meaningless ritualism and other practices so common in Hindu modes of worship. He succeeded in initiating much enlightened thought on religious practices and his influence spread widely among many sections of the Hindu community. His stay in this country lasted nearly five years with a brief interruption of a few months to visit India.

Swami Shankarananda was the first Hindu monk ever to visit South Africa. His visit occurred at a very significant period in South Africa's history. Less than two years after his arrival the four provinces were united to form the Union of South Africa and exactly two years after this he brought the South African Hindu Maha Sabha into existence—on 31st May 1912.[10] The Swami's knowledge of Hindu Philosophy enabled him to speak on the subject in many centres. In Johannesburg the Mayor of the city was elected Chairman of the Reception Committee, which accorded him a fitting welcome there. He delivered a series of about twenty lectures in the Masonic Hall, which so impressed people as to draw large crowds of non-Hindu, particularly white, audiences. The Governor of Natal, Sir Mathew Nathan became a close friend of the Swami.[11]

The Swami's talks were aimed at pinpointing which ritualistic practices he disagreed with. It is significant that ritualistic Hinduism had become the sole repository of religious practice for a large number of Hindus in India and elsewhere. And since people like Swami Shankarananda were committed to new systems of practice, his attacks were aimed mainly at removing what he and many Arya Samajists considered irrelevant, if not meaningless, religious practice. Pandit Nardev is of the view that the Swami's particular approach lay in making a sermonic appeal for the proper observation of festivals, daily prayers *(Saṁskāras)* and the study of the vernacular.[12] Following Swami Shankarananda's original appeal, which he repeated many times, many people developed a new religious awareness. The average Hindu very often sees the study of religion as synonymous with the speaking of an Indian language. He formed several small organisations of which the Veda Dharma Sabha of Pietermaritzburg flourishes to this day.[13]

The Swami's greatest wish was to spread the gospel of the Arya Samaj. It was expected on his arrival here that his work would be directed at this and he is always remembered for that contribution in this country. Swami Shankarananda is also remembered, however, for one outstanding contribution to Hinduism in South Africa, namely the formation of the South African Hindu Maha Sabha, which represents Hindu religio-cultural interests nationally.[14] In May 1987 the Maha Sabha celebrated its seventy-fifth anniversary in Durban—the city of its birth.[15]

The Swami's tour of South Africa, particularly his visit to the Transvaal, was aimed at preaching the gospel of Hinduism as he understood it. His preoccupation with preaching Hinduism pure and simple brought him into conflict with Mahatma Gandhi, who was living in South Africa at the time and was deeply involved in the political struggles of the Indian people. His political campaigning involved uniting Hindu and Muslim people. For Swami Shankarananda, the pain and agony arising from the desecration of India and Hinduism with the mass conversion of millions of Hindus to Islam lingered on. However, his primary concern was with the regeneration of national, cultural and religious pride. The Swami saw his spiritual ministry in the context of the reawakening of pride in his people which he felt was sorely lacking.[16]

The results of Swami Shankarananda's ministry were felt in two directions. Firstly, there was the re-establishment of pride in religion, culture and language and secondly there was the attempt to enthuse people with high moral standards of behaviour in all walks of life. The impact that the Swami made on the people was naturally limited to his sphere of contact which varied in the cities and depended largely on the way people responded to invitations to attend his talks. The Swami proved himself to be a good friend and teacher of great merit among all with whom he came into contact.

Swami Bhawani Dayal was by all accounts the first and best known Arya Samajist born in South Africa. He was born in Johannesburg on 10 September 1892.[17] Although his contribution to Indian life and thought is remembered in political circles it is as an Āryaṇ missionary that he is mostly appreciated. Deeply committed to the Arya Samaj cause, he worked as tirelessly for it when the opportunity came, as he did for the political emancipation of his people in India and South Africa. Swami Bhawani Dayal, as a political activist, courted arrest for several offences committed under the numerous Acts passed by the Government to deliberately frustrate the Indian community. It was during these political troubles that Mahatma Gandhi led his people from political subjugation. He was assisted by many Indian stalwarts, Swami Bhawani Dayal being one of his closest friends and associates.

Bhawani Dayal chose to become a monk during one of his early visits to India.[18] After the death of his wife he joined a holy order and was given the name Swami Bhawani Dayal Sannyāsi. On his return to South Africa he based his work on the Arya Samaj ideal, with the spread of the Hindi language as its pivot of religious reform. As a preacher of the Vedic message he toured Natal and the Transvaal with a deep desire to reform Hindu society, particularly the Hindi-speaking people. He delivered many lectures and performed many ceremonies including the well-known *Śuddhī Saṁskāra*, whereby converts from Hinduism were reconverted to their original faith.

The Swami was involved in a plethora of religious and political activities which took up much of his time. His life thus became a constant dedication to the cause and wherever he went it was either as a religious missionary or a political one. His ideal was however the emancipation of his people, firstly from political oppression and secondly from immature thinking on religious matters which he saw as rife in the Hindi community in Natal.

Swami Bhawani Dayal's dedication to the Aryan cause was in a sense the foundation for the promotion of the Arya Samaj movement.[19] The minds of many were tuned to the idea of it being built on solid and constructive ideals. Thus the Swami's interest in the life and work of Swami Dayananda Sarasvati earned for him in 1925 the position of Chairman of the Centenary Celebration Committee, formed to mark the birth of the leader of the Arya Samaj in India. It naturally followed that this position was going to be followed by a more lasting and honoured one, as president of the Arya Pratinidhi Sabha when it came into existence in South Africa.

The teachers whose brief biographies we have traced thus far in this section were the men who laid the foundations of the Arya Pratinidhi Sabha of South Africa in the years prior to its formation in 1925. It was not until many years later that the movement's greatest servant came to this country and built it into an organisation of great merit.

Pandit Nardev Vedalankar was originally invited to South Africa as a teacher of Gujarati. His arrival here in 1947 was awaited with much enthusiasm and it was known that his contribution to the study of Hindi, Arya Samaj ideals and modern Hinduism would receive great attention. It was intended that he would stay for five years. His services to the Arya Samaj cause now span forty years and he still maintains the position with untarnished esteem and appreciation.

Many members of the Hindu community are appreciative of the fact that Pandit Nardev, a graduate of the Gurukul at Kangri, who is a Gujarati-speaking person, had dedicated himself to the teaching of Gujarati and Hindi. He was one of those responsible for the coming into existence of the Hindi Shiksha Sangha, which has been responsible for much Hindi education in Natal. The Hindi Shiksha Sangha is a cultural organisation that has been responsible for "awakening cultural interest in young people in the Hindi community in this country." Since the formation of the Hindi Shiksha Sangha and its affiliates in many parts of Natal, interest in Hindi education and culture has grown very widely. Its members have taken to the performing arts and the annual eisteddfod attracts very wide attention.

It is estimated that there are over fifty branches of the Sangha, which is now styled the Hindi Shiksha Sangha of South Africa. Many hundreds, young and old, participate in these annual eisteddfods with their numerous sections of artistic talent in which people compete for honours. Pandit Nardev is one of the chief architects of this achievement. The organisation is not confined to Arya Samajists. Many non-Arya Samajists participate in its work and the organisation attracts a very wide following of people drawn from the Hindi community.

Pandit Nardev was for some time a member of staff at the University of Durban-Westville, where he taught Gujarati. The author of several works on Hinduism, he is still the spiritual adviser to the Arya Pratinidhi Sabha of South Africa.

Panditji's contribution to the growth and development of Hinduism lies in two areas of learning: faith in the Department in which he works as adviser and Ācārya to the Arya Pratinidhi Sabha. He is also president of the Veda Niketan which is responsible for publishing several works on Hinduism. Hindi is the national language of India and Panditji's ideal, like that of many Indians, is that it be spoken by as many people of Indian origin as possible.

He is also Chairman of the Vedic Purohit Mandal, which seeks to inculcate and develop the study and practice of Vedic Saṁskāras (ceremonies). Priests of both sexes are trained for this purpose and to date no less than thirty have been ordained to conduct religious services.

REFERENCES

1. Vedalankar, N., et Somera, M., *Arya Samaj and Indians Abroad*, Arya Pratinidhi Sabha, Durban, 1975.
2. Vedalankar, N., *Religious Awakening in South Africa*, Arya Pratinidhi Sabha, Durban, 1950.
3. "The Rising Sun", Vol. 1 No. 3.
4. Vedalankar, et Somera, *Ibid.*
5. Vedalankar, N., *Ibid.*
6. Vedalankar, N., *Ibid.*
7. Souvenir Brochure: Ved Dharma Sabha, Pietermaritzburg, 1960.
8. Annual Report, 1950. Arya Pratinidhi Sabha, Durban, 1950.
9. Desai, N.P., *History of the South African Hindu Maha Sabha*, Hindu Maha Sabha (Publishers), Durban, 1960.
10. Desai, N.P., *Ibid.*
11. Vedalankar, N., *Ibid.*
12. Souvenir Brochure: Ved Dharma Sabha Pietermaritzburg, 1960.
13. Souvenir Brochure: Ved Dharma Sabha Pietermaritzburg, 1960.
14. Desai, N.P., *Ibid.*
15. Naidoo, T. ed. *Challenge*: Papers presented at Hindu Convention, S.A. Hindu Maha Sabha, Durban, 1982.
16. Naidoo, T., *Ibid.*
17. Agrawal, P.N., *Bhawani Dayal Sannyasi*, Indian Colonial Association, Durban.
18. Agrawal, P.N., *Ibid.*
19. Hindi Shiksha Sangha, Annual Report, Durban, 1982.

CHAPTER 3

Arya Pratinidhi Sabha of South Africa

THE YEAR 1925 marked the centenary of the birth of Swami Dayananda Sarasvati. Hindu communities in at least ten countries observed the occasion with various celebrations and festivities.[1] South Africa's Hindu community, particularly its Hindi-speaking people, celebrated with equal enthusiasm. That the occasion should be observed in South Africa arose from suggestions made by several people to whom the life and work of Swami Dayananda was well-known. An organisation known as the Arya Yuvak Sabha, which had been in existence for several years and which was designed to preach the Arya Samaj doctrine, had prepared for the celebrations to be marked with due ceremony.[2] Preliminary discussions revealed considerable enthusiasm and the growing interest in the Arya Samaj and its establishment in this country soon became an important talking point. A meeting was held in Durban on 22 November 1924, at which it was decided that Śivarātri day in 1925 should be observed in South Africa with the attention it deserved.[3] A weeklong series of celebrations was held, and at the last meeting, on 22 February 1925, Śivarātri day, the Arya Pratinidhi Sabha of South Africa came into existence.[4] This was exactly one hundred years after the birth of the founder of the Indian movement and fifty years to the day after the movement itself was formed in India.

The birth of the Arya Pratinidhi Sabha was not the beginning of the work of the Arya Samaj movement in South Africa. It was one very significant milestone in its history. For many years previously the work of Prof. Bhai Parmanand, Swami Shankarananda, Swami Bhawani Dayal and other prominent Arya Samajists was being propagated.[5] In addition, organisations such as the Arya Yuvak Sabha and the Veda Dharma Sabha of Pietermaritzburg had been in existence to propagate Arya Samaj principles and ideals. In fact the First Conference,[6] at which the Arya Pratinidhi Sabha was formed, was attended by 136 delegates from the following organisations who concurred that the formation of the Arya Pratinidhi Sabha was necessary for co-ordinating and unifying the work of the various organisations already existing and which were represented at this conference.[7] These organisations were:

i. Arya Yuvak Sabha—Durban
ii. Arya Hindi Ashram—Clare Estate
iii. Satya Vedic Dharma Jigyasi Sabha—Cato Manor
iv. Hindi Pracharni Sabha—Sydenham
v. Arya Samaj—Ladysmith
vi. Hindu Young Men's Association—Newcastle
vii. Hindu Young Men's Association—Pietermaritzburg
viii. Vidya Pracharni Sabha—Pietermaritzburg
ix. Veda Dharma Sabha—Pietermaritzburg
x. Vidya Pracharni Sabha—Rooikopjes
xi. Young Men's Society—Point
xii. Nagari Pracharni Sabha—Springfield
xiii. Arya Yuvak Mandal—Sea Cow Lake
xiv. Vedic Sarmangi Sabha—Umgeni
xv. Agri Pracharni Sabha—Camp Drift

Several significant features of the meeting form part of the historical development of the organisation. Firstly, the South African Hindu Maha Sabha, which was formed in 1910, lay dormant and little could be done to resuscitate it.[8] It had actually been formed to represent the religious and cultural aspirations of the entire Hindu community in the country. Its dormancy caused people to rethink its ability to represent the Hindu community. The formation of the Arya Pratinidhi Sabha, although primarily intended to represent Arya Samaj interests nationwide also had to fill the gap left by the Maha Sabha.

The resolution passed at the meeting on 22 February 1925 to give birth to the Arya Pratinidhi Sabha read: "For the purpose of preaching the tenets of the Vedic Religion a body named Central Aryan Vedic Society"[9] be formed. An amendment to the resolution, however read: "The delegates attending the Rishi Dayanand Centenary Celebration resolve to establish an Arya Pratinidhi Sabha through whose medium the cause of Vedic Religion be advanced."[10] The Arya Pratinidhi Sabha then became a reality.[11]

The second feature of note is that seven important resolutions were passed at this historic conference. These were:[12]

i. Abstinence from indulgence in alcoholic drinks.
ii. Performance of 16 Saṁskāras.
iii. Reciting Sandhyā prayers and havan daily.
iv. Holding feelings of love and brotherhood for all people.
v. Removal of the caste system.
vi. The encouragement of mother tongue education.
vii. Education for women and girls.

After the establishment of the Arya Pratinidhi Sabha it was decided to affiliate it to the Sarvadeshik Arya Pratinidhi Sabha (International Aryan League) of India. This affiliation took place on 23 October 1927.[13]

Soon after the formation of the Arya Pratinidhi Sabha the officials of the organisation set about trying to achieve the ideals they set for themselves. Since its inception the Arya Pratinidhi Sabha has held numerous Vedic Conferences to engender interest in the Hindu community.[14] These conferences, each of national significance, were organised as part of the programme of reconstruction dealing with particular aspects of Hindu life and thought in South Africa.

The first Vedic Conference, that brought into existence the Arya Pratinidhi Sabha,[15] was held on 16 February 1925. The second was held in Ladysmith on 3 October in the same year and brought together many Hindu organisations for discussion on common problems.[16] Over the weekend of the 31 July and 1 August of the following year the third conference was held, the fourth in March 1939, the fifth over two days in February 1942 and the sixth on 19 July 1947.[17]

The Arya Pratinidhi Sabha was responsible for convening the first ever Hindu youth conference in South Africa.[18] This was held in Durban on 31 July 1948, when various speakers delivered papers of cultural and religious significance.

In July 1944, the Sabha convened a conference of priests at which matters concerning the methods to be employed in the performance of ritual ceremonies were discussed and some important decisions concerning these were taken.[19]

The Sabha also convened further meetings to discuss children's education, the institution of Hindi as the common language among all Hindus, and events in the life of Swami Dayananda Sarasvati such as his birth anniversary, death anniversary, etc.[20]

Ever since the formation of the Arya Pratinidhi Sabha, the desire was expressed among many of its members that the movement needed premises to house its headquarters. Ten years after its inception, the organisation was able, through the generous efforts of some of its leading members, to purchase property in the heart of the central business district of the city of Durban and plans were soon mooted for the building of a physical structure to house the organisation's headquarters.[21] It came in the form of an old building situated at 21 Carlisle Street, Durban purchased on 1 April 1936.[22] This building was used for many years until many well-meaning philanthropists contributed to the building of the Vedic Temple and hall which were completed in 1975 in its place. The construction of this building meant that the Society, although not seriously handicapped by the use of the older building existing on the site, at the time of purchase, now found it sufficiently commodious to conduct its affairs with far greater facility than before.[23]

The opening of the Temple in October 1975 marked the society's fiftieth year of existence,[24] and the occasion was celebrated with due pomp and ceremony. A brochure marking this Golden Jubilee gives ample evidence of the joy of the occasion, with many notable personalities joining in the celebrations.[25] Two Ācāryas from India, specially invited to the celebrations, which culminated in many people in Durban, other parts of Natal and even in the rest of South Africa coming to recognise the existence of the institution started in the name of reformed Hinduism. The physical structure is a good example of an Indian building with the facade bearing a Hindu motif. Great difficulties were experienced in raising the necessary funds, but when these were overcome, members were able to settle down to putting to use the Vedic Temple and hall (built at a cost of about Rs. 160000). The Arya Pratinidhi Sabha was thus able to commemorate the centenary of the founding of the Indian movement, and the fiftieth anniversary of its own formation in a building entirely its own, free of debt and large enough for the programme of work decided by its founding fathers.[26]

My attendance at meetings, firstly a meeting of the Executive Council of the Sabha at its headquarters and secondly the 58th Annual General Meeting held on 24 April 1983, was well received. There was much discussion about the Centenary of the death of Swami Dayananda Sarasvati. In this regard the programmes of service and commemorative meetings envisaged were very numerous, indicating the nature of the efforts to publicise the life and work of the founder of the movement.[27]

The fifty-seventh annual report of the Sabha[28] contains information on its activities. Its fifty-seven years of existence reflect steady and progressive involvement in specific areas of service which may be measured and assessed only over a long period of time. The report however demarcates special services rendered in ritual ceremonies: weddings, funerals, and "other saṁskāras".[29] It also lists the names of festivals like Śivarātri, which in the Arya Samaj movement is referred to as "Dayananda Enlightenment Day", Ram Naumi, Kṛṣṇa Aṣḥtamī, Dīpāvalī and a few minor observances.

The prayer meetings at the Vedic Temple are held once every week. The Sabha is very anxious also that other services which are conducted at local prisons and elsewhere be encouraged in every way. The annual meeting took note of the enormous service being rendered by the Arya Samaj movement to religious awakening in South Africa among the Hindu community. The publication of a newsletter is a recent innovation giving a strong indication of the effort to publicise the work of the Samaj so far as Swami Dayananda's life and work are concerned.

The work of the Arya Pratinidhi Sabha is no longer centred at its headquarters. Much attention is given to its multi-faceted activities in its subsidiary organisations in all parts of Natal which are engaged in numerous activities closely connected with the social, cultural and, above all, religious upliftment of the Hindu community.

REFERENCES

1. Vedalankar, N., et Somera, M., *Arya Samaj and Indians Abroad*, Sarvadeshik APS, Delhi, 1975.
2. Vedalankar, N., *Ibid.*
3. Vedalankar, N., *Ibid.*
4. Vedalankar, N., *Ibid.*
5. Agarwal, P.N., *Ibid.*
6. *Arya Yuvak Sabha, Annual Report, 1940*
7. *Arya Yuvak Sabha, Annual Report, 1940*
8. *Vedalankar, N., Ibid.*
9. Annual Report, Arya Pratinidhi Sabha, Durban, 1950.
10. Annual Report, Arya Pratinidhi Sabha, Durban, 1950.
11. Annual Report, Arya Pratinidhi Sabha, Durban, 1950.
12. Annual Report, Arya Pratinidhi Sabha, Durban, 1950.
13. Annual Report, Arya Pratinidhi Sabha, Durban, 1950.
14. Vedalankar, N., *Ibid.*

15. Arya Pratinidhi Sabha,Report, 1955.
16. Arya Pratinidhi Sabha,Report, 1955.
17. Arya Pratinidhi Sabha,Report, 1955.
18. Vedalankar, N., *Ibid.*
19. Annual Report, Vedic Purohit Mandal, Durban, 1960.
20. Annual Report, Arya Yuvak Sabha, Durban, 1965
21. Annual Report, Arya Pratinidhi Sabha, Durban, 1940.
22. Golden Jubilee 1925-1975 Brochure, Arya Pratinidhi Sabha, Durban, 1975.
23. *Ibid.*
24. *Ibid.*
25. *Ibid.*
26. *Ibid.*
27. Annual Meeting: Arya Pratinidhi Sabha, Durban, 1983.
28. Annual Report and Financial Statement, Arya Pratinidhi Sabha, 1981.
29. Report presented to meeting of Arya Pratinidhi Sabha.

CHAPTER 4

Aims and Objects

SWAMI DAYANANDA founded the Arya Samaj in 1875 with the aim of promoting the spiritual, social and physical well-being of all mankind.[1] That the Arya Samaj chose, at least as a stated principle, to work for "all mankind" is significant and theoretically typifies its universal outlook. Arya Samaj work has however always been confined to Hindu society and its moral, social, political and primarily religious objectives. The Arya Samaj has therefore chosen to divide "Mankind" into two groups, namely people it regards as noble at least in outlook and behaviour and those less inclined to living by noble principles. The Arya Samaj message is thus aimed at upholding principles that span a variety of ideals for human welfare. Pandit Nardev[2] has discussed these under the following headings:

i. Philosophical and spiritual ideals;
ii. Outlook towards the world;
iii. Ethically disciplined life;
iv. Development of individuality;
v. Development of social consciousness; and
vi. World unity and universal brotherhood.[3]

The Ṛg Vedic assertion that all should aim to be noble is used as Vedic authority for such a principle. Thus the word Ārya itself always implies nobility and transcends sect, race, colour or creed. The Arya Samaj thus obviates an important difficulty that could arise by claiming that all people, irrespective of race or nationality, could be Arya Samajists. The Society seeks only to bring together "pure, noble and righteous persons".[4] It therefore concludes that people of all nations could be Arya Samajists provided they respect the culture and religious sovereignty of other nations. It is for this reason that many non-Hindus also respected Swami Dayananda.

Nobility of outlook had thus become a fundamental article of faith. Arya Samajists believed this had been lacking among Christians and Muslims in particular, as evidenced by missionary achievements in India before the coming of Swami Dayananda. Missionary work was based on narrow principles which enforced conversion, lack of religious tolerance and above all religious bigotry of the very worst kind.[5]

The universality of outlook to which the Arya Samaj subscribes has of necessity to be upheld largely as a theoretical principle. These very principles had necessarily to be submerged until Hindu ideals as conceived by the Arya Samaj were raised to a more lasting and recognisable level. The spiritual principles to which the Arya Samaj subscribes therefore speak of the broadest of Hindu teachings to accommodate its subscription to universality. These are:[6]

a. Its belief in one God as the father of all mankind.
b. God-realisation as the aim of life.
c. And belief that it is possible to know God through the knowledge of the Vedas revealed by God "at the beginning of the universe for all mankind".

The Arya Pratinidhi Sabha is fully aware of the need for a wide catholicity of views but the aims and objectives of the Sabha are more strictly defined for the sake of Hindu unity. Before 1925, several Hindu organisations had been in existence, some of them preaching Arya Samaj principles.[7] The tours of this country by people like Swami Shankarananda, Professor Bhai Parmananda and Swami Bhawani Dayal served to inspire people to think in terms of Hindu unity and service to the community in respect of Hindu cultural and religious ideals.[8]

The seven main aims of the Arya Pratinidhi Sabha, as listed in its constitution are:[9]

i. To establish, organise and consolidate Arya Samaj institutions and Vedic societies in South Africa.
ii. To preach the Arya Samaj and its Ten Principles in this country.
iii. To disseminate the Vedic religion and philosophy.
iv. To promote the art, culture and civilization of India.
v. To encourage and advocate the study and use of Hindi and other Indian languages.
vi. To protect and defend the rights of Hindus and to concern itself with their spiritual, moral and social upliftment.
vii. To co-operate with other Hindu organisations on matters affecting the Hindu community.

The constitution goes on to stipulate that the headquarters of the Arya Pratinidhi Sabha shall be situated at 21 Carlisle Street, at the large building complex which houses the Vedic Temple, the Aryan Hall and the Bhawani Dayal Council Chamber. In 1973 a historical account of the Sabha was published,[10] in which it was stated that twenty-six institutions "working on the basis of Arya Samaj principles and Vedic ideals" were affiliated to the Arya Pratinidhi Sabha. The annual report for 1981[11] lists the names and addresses of forty-three institutes then affiliated to it.

The Arya Pratinidhi Sabha has now been in existence for sixty-three years. In the year 1983 Arya Samajists all over the world marked the centenary of the death of Swami Dayananda the founder of their movement. In South Africa, several of the more erstwhile members of the organisation look back on sixty years of service to the community. It is however regarded sometimes as small and insignificant and often criticized for not strictly conforming to all the Arya Samaj rules laid down by its founder.[12]

Almost all the members and supporters of the Arya Pratinidhi Sabha are Hindi-speaking and all religious and cultural ties are irrevocably measured against love for Hindi. So, "one of the main activities of the affiliated units has been the establishment of classes and the building of schools for the imparting of Hindi education".[13] The educational needs of the Hindu community gave rise to concerted efforts being made to imparting Hindi education to Hindu children.

REFERENCES

1. Vedalankar, N., *Arya Samaj—Its Ideals and Achievements*, Veda Niketan, Durban, 1975, p. 24.
2. Vedalankar, N., *Ibid*, p. 8.
3. Vedalankar, N., *Ibid*. p. 8.
4. Chotia, S., *Arya Pratinidhi Sabha—Historical Account*, Veda Niketan, Durban, 1973.
5. *Ibid.*
6. Annual Report Arya Pratinidhi Sabha.
7. *Ibid.*
8. Constitution: Arya Pratinidhi Sabha.
9. Chotia, S. *Ibid.*
10. Annual Report and Financial Statement 1981, Arya Pratinidhi Sabha.
11. Annual Report, APS, 1980.
12. Annual Report, Hindi Shiksha Sangha.
13. Annual Report, Hindi Shiksha Sangha.

CHAPTER 5

Reception and Dialogue

THE RECEPTION accorded the Arya Samaj by the Hindu community, although by and large enthusiastic and supportive, was also at times hostile.[1] The Hindu community, and to a lesser extent the Gujarati community, was split into two camps, one supportive and the other antagonistic. An interview with Mr. N.M. revealed one of the most important reasons for the attitudes of intransigence which characterised dialogue between the two groups. It was during this time that the two terms "Samajists" and "Sanatanis" came into vogue to distinguish representatives of the two factions. Most people found themselves very unwilling to place their age-old religious beliefs and traditions on the sacrificial altar of reform.

The establishment of the Arya Pratinidhi Sabha was therefore greeted with some trepidation. Although the Samajists were very enthusiastic about it, Sanatanis displayed some reserve, and in some instances opposition. The work of the Arya Yuvak Sabha and the Ved Dharma Sabha for more than a decade prior to the establishment of the parent organisation had already spread suspicion and animosity among the community generally.[2] Sanatanis, however, felt uneasy about the Arya Pratinidhi Sabha because of its enthusiasm to spread its gospel.

The formation of the Arya Pratinidhi Sabha thus served as a catalyst for thinking among Sanatanis about their own religious position. It was not until April 1941, however, that they were able to give expression to their aspirations through the formation of a national organisation called the Shree Sanatan Dharma Sabha of South Africa.[3] Although the Sanatan Dharma Sabha was supposed to represent the majority of people in the Hindu community and also the more conservative and orthodox viewpoint, it was never established that it actually had as strong an influence over the Hindu people as the Arya Samaj had.

The establishment of Shree Sanatan Dharma Sabha had one serious effect on the Hindu community in its concern for religious practice. The open discussions between the two groups often escalated into serious verbal and theological battles on the essential basis of religious affiliation for the Hindu people. Articles in newspapers such as "The Leader" and "The Rising Sun" bore testimony to this conflict of ideas which was so strongly felt in the Hindu community.[4] The feelings have always engendered and maintained the division with readers still publicising their respective stands in the "The Leader" and other newspapers. In an article published in this newspaper in 1982, reference was made to the controversy that raged through its columns on the merits of the caste system and other matters that affected the Hindu community at the time of the formation of the Arya Pratinidhi Sabha, 40 years earlier and their persistence in South Africa even at the present time.[5] This is however not to suggest that the two organisations have remained opposed to each other on theological and other grounds and no meeting for consensus could ever be arranged. Not so. Another correspondent's letter to 'The Leader', published in the same edition, drew attention to the efforts made by some members of both organisations, deeply affected by the rift the controversy causes within the community to heal the rift in every way possible.[6] One example of this is that the "anniversary celebrations of the Shri Vishnu Temple were characterised by close participation between Arya Samaj and Sanatan persons..."[7]

Despite these efforts on the part of members of both groups the rift remains, although it is never allowed to interfere with the work of the Arya Samaj, which is committed to its own programme of action.[8]

An interview with two senior officials of the Shree Sanatan Dharma Sabha elicited the long-standing views held by Sanatanis generally. The first interviewee was of the view that a mūrti (idol) symbolised the living God in concrete form. Although Arya Samajists, he said, did not believe in Mūrtis, they had no right to show disrespect to the Mūrti that Sanatanis have in their temples. Sanatanis he said believed in visualising an image of God when they felt the need to do so. Thus worship for them is worship through symbols because symbols have an important part to play in all worship. The very language Sanatanis use in worship, the symbol Om, the songs and all rituals symbolise worship and add concrete form to it. Thus devotion to God is only complete when it becomes devotion to a symbol, or a form. Although images may be in stone or wood, to Sanatanis they represent God with form. Without the central deity a temple is empty and ordinary people who have no profound understanding of God or the Hindu religion are never inspired by an empty Temple. But a Temple filled with images represents a cultural and religious tradition richly blessed. An Arya Samaj Temple is known for its emptiness and coldness, and many worshippers have difficulty in placing it into a specific cultural mould.

A strong controversy that still exists is the problem surrounding the Vedas. Sanatanis are generally reluctant to accept Swami Dayananda's view or interpretation of them. They are prepared to grant some validity to his arguments but are reluctant to grant him total authority.

They believe that Dayananda's views concerning the Purāṇas are his personal views. Sanatanis are not obliged to accept or follow them. They are of the view that the Purāṇas do not contradict the Vedas, but uphold them. They support them and even interpret them for the devotee's benefit. While Sanatanis are aware of Swami Dayananda's condemnation of the Purāṇas with some justification, they are not insensitive to the part played by the Purāṇas in preserving Hinduism, even in "adulterated" form. For this Sanatanis are grateful. They therefore do not deny the authority of the Vedas, but are also grateful to the Purāṇas for the good they have done while not unmindful of the difficulties that arise with their study.

The second interviewee believed that Arya Samajists generally displayed strong attitudes of dogmatism and that such attitudes did little to engender religious tolerance and harmony for which Hinduism is well-known. Hindu missionaries have always seen much good in the religion of the Sanatanis, and many Hindus are convinced that there is no dire need for such a radical transformation of modes of worship and religious practice as advocated by the Arya Samaj. The Sanatanis' contention therefore is that Arya Samajists should broaden their outlook on religious practice. While many people are appreciative of their viewpoint and are impressed with the good that results from it, one has to be aware of their dogmatism and narrowness of outlook. But Sanatanis are particularly proud of the contributions made by the Brahmin community in upholding culture and religion and preserving it for the benefit of Hindus of later generations.

It would appear from the interview that some attempt at dialogue was made and while both groups of people were aware of each other's viewpoint, no compromise seemed possible.

Sanatanis in South Africa are aware of Swami Dayananda's style of discussion, as exemplified by the discussion between him and Sanatanis at Meerut.[9] It appears that his unwillingness to refrain from denouncing idolatry was one of the most important reasons for Sanatanis rejecting him. It was also clear that despite Swami Dayananda's open rejection of the contention that his preaching was a form of "Dayanandism", many Sanatanis remain unconvinced of Dayananda's statement: "It is wrong for anyone of you to say that you believe in the religion of Dayananda. What you should say is that your religion is Vedic."[10] Sanatanis are also reluctant to believe that Dayananda had an absolutely clear grasp of the Vedas in the first place.

A further problem with Sanatanis is their difficulty in understanding his respect for all religions of the world while failing to see any good in Sanatanist doctrines. The Sanatani standpoint is that if any man claims to respect all religions in the world it is difficult to understand why he does not respect all traditions and sects within Hinduism itself. Some Sanatanis were also not unmindful of the fact that *Satyartha Prakash* was highly critical of Christianity and Islam. Although Sanatanis feel that this criticism is not unjustified, his criticism of Jainism and Sikhism they felt extended beyond the limits of scholarly investigation.

In this respect J.N. Farquhar[11] observes that the Arya Samaj has often encouraged antagonism and Dayananda's methods succeeded in arousing many sects to retaliation. This observation was not absent from the reception Arya Samaj received in South Africa. Sanatanis, however, appreciate the stand taken by the Arya Samaj on matters that have for centuries plagued Hinduism and therefore welcome Dayananda's role as a reformer. For example, orthodox Hinduism allows only men of the three higher castes to study the Vedas. The Arya Samaj innovation in inviting both men and women of all castes to study them is accepted with the one single proviso that it has always been a Hindu tradition to allow only, in Arya Samaj terms, Aryas to study them. Sanatanis now concede that Hinduism's greatest mistake was to have given importance to Brahminism. The new religion of the Arya Samaj says that only Aryas should study the Vedas. This means even Harijans if they display sufficient interest and spiritual inclination for it.

The formation of the two organisations within the Hindu community was responsible for the cleavage in religious commitment. This dichotomy has engendered a crisis of conscience which has persisted to the present day and no clear statement was ever made by either group to allay fears and satisfy desires for the theological reconciliation that many have sought. Two works that have tried to bring forth in clearer terms the viewpoints of both sects have done little to reconcile their respective stands.[12] However the important feature of this is, unfortunate as it may appear for those who wish to encourage a cohesive and united community, that while both organisations do everything to encourage their own theological perspectives, they also encourage deeper religious commitment.

In so doing the Arya Samaj has been able to make the performance of *havan* fundamental to all worship within its own system. Every sacrament and every ritual has the *havan* as its most important sacrifice and Samajists thus reaffirm at every service their total commitment to a system of worship that has its origins in Vedic times. In so doing they believe themselves to be followers of the religion of the Vedas and preserve its most sacred ideals in every way possible.[13]

Sanatanis, on the other hand, sing songs dedicated to the many personages of the Hindu tradition. They encourage the chanting of *Hanumān Cālisa*, which has grown in popularity over the years. With the formation of the two large Vedantic institutions in South Africa,[14] the chanting of *Hanumān Cālisa* has become even more popular. Readings from *Rāmāyaṇa* and *Mahābhārata* grow in popularity and the study of all sacred literature grows with corresponding enthusiasm. While this is not done with any conscious effort at thwarting Arya Samaj interests it certainly helps to remind the Samaj that Hindu thinking is still firmly structured in a way that has been in vogue since Vedic times. Sanatanis therefore, also believe themselves to be followers of the religion of the Vedas.

We began this chapter by stating the intention to discuss the Samaj as a structural functional system of religious endeavour. We have so far come to recognise how the life and message of Swami Dayananda has been not only the inspiration behind the Arya Samaj movement but also the guiding hand behind the renaissance of Hinduism in South Africa. This must be seen against the important fact of the birth of this movement in a setting in which modern times were being experienced more clearly than in India. South Africa, a modern western industrialised country, provided a new environment in a new historical period for a growing neo-Hinduism. A fundamental condition for a dynamic society, which probably was Dayananda's intention, is the freedom to be religiously expressive and provide room for the growth and expression of religious endeavour in a new direction. Above all Samajic teachings gave scope for criticism of old values, determination of new ones within a changing social structure and finally effected a modernised constitutional framework for the growth and development of theological ideals in a reformed, modern context free of old superstitions and non-religious inanities.

Arya Samaj leaders in enforcing changes indicated their passion for new ideas. A passion accompanied by a willingness to suffer criticism through their initiation of the moves that effected the ultimate changes sought. The result has been a revival of Hinduism, but in a new form, with a religious movement advocating strong socio-ethical values and a reorientation of an ancient faith to meet new challenges in a modern age.[15]

The outstanding feature of this new movement, the pivot around which all other facets of its ideal revolve, is the belief that the Vedas, the treasury of science and morals, were revealed by God for man's illumination.[16] Dayananda regarded their textual portion as self-evident truth, admitting of no doubt and depending on the authority of no other book. Commentaries on the Vedas, such as the Brāhmaṇas, were considered authentic because they adhered to conceptual models in the Vedas. If they departed even slightly from Vedic Truth their authority as scripture would be diminished.

The Vedas are viewed as scriptural ideals which advocate the speaking of truth. Truth and justice are regarded as important values among others that enhance religious endeavour that leads to final illumination.

The soul, immortal and invisible, is endowed with the ability to think and judge. It is also affected by desire and passion, pleasure and pain. God and soul are incorporeal and unchangeable and are related to each other as the pervader is to the pervaded. The distinction of their respective individualisation is constant, which means that their physical natures are not identical. Divine power is the cause of creation and the equitable bestower of rewards and punishments on the actions of souls. Creation points to a Creator, while birth and death are to be seen as springing from ignorance which perpetrates irreligious acts, which in turn promote the worship of objects instead of God.

Salvation is the state of emancipation from pain and subjection to birth and death and equal to a life of liberty and happiness in the immensity of God. The means of salvation are contemplation of God, abstraction of mind, practice of virtue, purity of thought, firmness of courage and love of knowledge.[17]

A superordinate meaning system envelopes the movement and engenders coherence in the hierarchical relationship of action and religio-social interchange. The existential referents of theoretical symbolism may be classified in terms of the empirical expressions within the movement. This enables us to grasp how the religious symbolism, in a phenomenological sense, reveals to the Arya Samajist his approach to the deepest aspects of reality.

Milton Yinger,[18] quoting Charles Clack and Rodney Stark, refers to religious beliefs, practices, knowledge and consequences within religious dimensions in experiential terms. Religious values he defines as attributes with possible variations permitting an adequate measurement of religion and religious behaviour. A difficulty arising from the effort to measure religious behaviour is the inter-connection between religious tradition and experiential verbalisation. Thus Dayananda's contention that Truth represents the highest value may represent for Arya Samajists an ideal by which the symbol is identified and formulates for them a plan of action.

The plan of action for Arya Samaj within its own definitional purview is bound to the domain of finite understanding. Unlike the ideal circumscribed by other systems within Hinduism, for example as may be described by Sri Ramakrishna, Dayananda's definitions are limited to religious endeavour in moral and ethical bounds. Sri Ramakrishna's "A man's duty is to be united with God", does not find a clear equivalent in Dayananda's expressions. "It is to know that God is the only Reality and that all else is unreal."[19] Sri Ramakrishna's illustrations of the means for unity between man and God have set the model for the ideal within the movement established by Swami Vivekananda.[20] Arya Samajic ideals are not described in clear expletives in experiential terms, but rather in ethical ideals. We thus find ourselves bound to the finite, the domain of the finite which symbols help to demarcate the highest truth through inductive expressions.

Arya Samajists nevertheless love Dayananda's expression concerning the *Tīrtha*, the religious ferry, the spiritual arc by which the sea of sorrow in the abyss of pain is crossed.[21] The Tīrthas are the speaking of truth, the attainment of knowledge, the friendship of savants, the practice of morality, dominion over the self, the discipline of mind, the magnanimity of heart, the instruction of science and the habit of beneficence. B.C. Singh lists the eight *gups* and eight true things that Arya Samajists are expected to avoid or follow.[22] The attainment of the ideal is the attainment of Reality in Arya Samaj terms. The aim lies in recognizing the all-pervading Spirit which transcends all limitations of human inadequacy and realising the goals rooted in Vedic Truth.

Smelser refers to this structural category of religious systematisation as situational facilities,[23] providing the means for facilitating religious attainments within specific contents. A specific medium provided by the Arya Samaj is the *Havan* ceremony; also adherence to the principles of Truth and other struggles as outlined in its ten principles. The Arya Samajist is expected to identify these and to incorporate them into the general frame of religious struggle which culminates in worship of the one true God of the Vedas. For Dayananda this indicated a more practical expression of religious struggle, which culminated in a more lasting religious experience, totally different from any that characterized traditional worship. The outstanding feature of this expression is response involving total being. The intensity of such involvement meant for Dayananda what Scheler described as religious cognition existing somewhat inadequately in theoretical definition, and only manifesting, when such involvement ends, in full expression of religious meaning.[24]

Religious liturgy within the Arya Samaj has necessarily to differ radically from Sanatani forms of worship. A specific pattern has therefore to be followed, emphasizing the religious constructs expressive of religion in action. Such action had necessarily to influence cultural behaviour whose effect is seen in the totality of expression within Hinduism. Religion is therefore a part of cultural fact. A design for living relative to sacred and ultimate things. As cultural fact it becomes part of social organisation. In the Durkheimian sense such social organisation unites those who share a body of beliefs while the individual is subject to beliefs and motives that incline him to total action. For the Arya Samajist action, while appearing as religion, finds its most meaningful expression in both religious and secular actions.

REFERENCES

1. This was the impression gained in several interviews with people familiar with the work of the Arya Samaj and the history of the movement.

2. Annual Report: Arya Yuvak Sabha, 1950.
3. Nowbath R.S., et al, *Hindu Heritage in South Africa*, Hindu Maha Sabha, Durban, 1960.
4. "The Leader", 4 September 1941.
5. "The Leader", 10 September 1982.
6. "The Leader", *Ibid.*
7. "The Rising Sun", *6 August 1938.*
8. "The Rising Sun", *Ibid.*.
9. Singh, B.C., *Life and Teachings of Swami Dayananda*, Jan Gyan Prakashan, Delhi, 1871.
10. Singh, B.C., *Ibid.*
11. Farquhar, J.N., *Modern Religious Movements in India*, Munshiram Manoharlal, Delhi,1977.
12. Bhawani Dayal, S., *Pravasi Ki Kahani*, Arya Pratinidhi Sabha, Durban, 1941.
13. Pande, S., *Murti Puja*, Sanatan Dharma Sabha, Natal, 1944.
14. The Ramakrishna Centre of South Africa. The Divine Life Society of South Africa.
15. Radhakrishnan, S., *Religion and Society*, Allen and Unwin, London, 1940, p. 63.
16. Radhakrishnan, S., *Religion and Society*,Allen and Unwin, London, p. 63.
17. Satya Prakash, S., *Dayananda's Vedic Philosophy*, Dayananda Sansthan, Delhi, 1975.
18. Yinger, M.J., *The Scientific Study of Religion*, MacMillan, London, 1970, p. 26.
19. Nikhilananda, S., *The Gospel of Sri Ramakrishna*, Ramakrishna Centre, New York, 1973, p. 579.
20. Gambhirananda, S., *The History of the Ramakrishna Math*, Advaita Ashram, Calcutta, 1936.
21. Singh, B.C., *Life of Dayananda*, p. 60.
22. Singh, B.C., *Ibid*, p. 60.
23. Smelser, J.N., *The Comparative Study of Religions*, pp. 97-98.
24. Scheler, M., *On the Eternal in Man*, p. 265.

SECTION FOUR

ARYA SAMAJ CONCEPT OF RELIGION

Introduction

THE FOUNDATIONS which Dayananda laid for the movement indicate firstly the depth of his spiritual convictions and secondly his depth of concern for Hindu society. The phenomenon of basic structures helps to distinguish within religion the complexities of religious types. Investigations into these circumstances of historical religions reveal the phenomenon that exposes the features of world religion or utilitarian modes and their appeal as God-centred folk lore.[1] Gustav Mensching distinguishes between folk religion and world religion and suggests that territorial diffusion is not the only distinguishing feature of such a distinction but rather also the deeper structural differentiation of religion per se.

For this reason it must be noted that the community becomes the vital carrier of a religion and its own responses to religious vitality help to restructure religious consciousness and religious purpose. In the analysis of world or, as is sometimes described, universal religion, external phenomena are inextricably associated with inner structures. Rudolf Otto's[2] "the law of parallels", is suggestive of the transition that occurs in certain situations and quite clearly the phenomenon is identified, as he says, in the transition from myth to logos, mythology to theology.

Dayananda's problem was precisely this. For him the transition from myth to logos was clearly one of the fundamental problems of Vedic exegesis, which was responsible for a burgeoning difficulty within Hindu theology. Its greatest difficulty undoubtedly lay in its failure to interpret and if necessary reinterpret Purāṇic lore, that hermeneutical ventures might be sustained at significant levels. Dayananda's problems lay quite clearly in the historical circumstances which lethargic Hinduism had engendered. Mensching's view that the transition from folk to universal religion occurred in every major religion may be true. His view that it occurred in India in 800 B.C. in the era of the Upaniṣads is accepted but also confirms that apart from the involvement of people like Śaṅkara and Rāmānuja, Hindu theology has remained largely unproductive and unaffected by fundamental changes in human existence.

Talcott Parsons[3] contends that in traditionalized higher cultures, religion tends to be mainly a conservative force; a balance wheel of society preventing departure from established ways. Dayananda's was the role of cleavage; from within the context of Hinduism it was necessary that stabilization had to be effected in terms of a totally new approach to an age-old theological format. Max Weber[4] believed that a traditional priestly class did not have great social power in classical Greece. This was a condition for Greek cultural activity. Conversely, this social ascendency of the Brahmin priestly caste in India before the coming of Dayananda is inseparable from the fact that Indian society is incontrovertably conservative and subsequently unyielding and unresponsive to creative theology.

The association of religion with the facts of social, economic and political stress and strain, even at the deepest levels of human life, makes it one of the main areas in which responses to situations are expected to be creative. Hindu society remains traditional and the traditions appear to be intermingled with tension and turmoil which remain largely unchanging. Dayananda's attempt at creative innovation for Hinduism and Hindu society was a period of dynamic religious development, as is evidenced by his work and influence after his death. That this contributed to much social turmoil, resulting in the deaths of many people despite his advocating *Śuddhi*, means that the peace the movement works for is unfortunately absent.

The foundations of the movement were well laid by Dayananda, setting its followers the task of orientating themselves to the visions of growth. The goals that Dayananda conceived and the values he supported are part of the programme the Samaj has now to follow and achieve. The keynote lies not in adaptation to emerging goals and values but mastery over them because of the very nature of religious activism.

REFERENCES

1. Mensching, G., *Folk and Universal Religion*, "Religion, Culture and Society" ed, Louis Schneider p. 254, John Wiley, New York, 1964.

2. Otto, R., *The Idea of the Holy*, Penguin, New York, 1959.

3. Parsons, T., *Religion as Creative Innovation, Religion, Society and the Individual*, ed "Yinger, M" p. 559, MacMillan, New York, 1950.

4. Weber, M., *The Religion of India, The Sociology of Hinduism and Buddhism*, ed and tr by Gerth, HH Martindale, D., Free Press, Glencoe Illinois, 1962.

CHAPTER 1

The Vedas as Authority for Arya Samaj Theology

DAYANANDA WAS adamant about the authority of the Vedas and saw this authority in the context of the superordinate meaningfulness assigned to them as Holy Scriptures, revealed as many Hindu scholars believe, "by God to man at the dawn of creation."[1] Dayananda saw the four Vedas as the repository of knowledge and religious truth, the very word of God. They comprised what he referred to as the *Saṁhitā Mantra Bhāg* and were for him absolutely free from error and the "Supreme and independent authority in all things."[2] He saw them as "self authoritative" and so all other books were dependent on them for authority.[3]

Swami Dayananda's interpretation of the Vedas and the importance he assigned to them as books of authority on Hindu life and thought is unique among teachers within the tradition. He assumed a most uncompromising stance on the nature of their authority: by seeing them as Supreme, Revealed Scriptures, the very fountainhead of the religious, cultural, educational, social and above all spiritual life of the Hindus. His most important and abiding intention was to formulate a philosophy, more correctly a theology, that would confirm his belief in their supremacy and which would form the basis from which all other facets of life could find doctrinal expression. He therefore made the slogan "Back to the Vedas" a sort of battle cry, because he believed that since their revelation at the dawn of creation many men in the Indian tradition had been inspired by them and in ages yet to come many others would follow who would be similarly moved.[4]

It was Swami Dayananda's firm belief that the decay and rot of degenerative Hinduism came about as a result of a general failure on the part of Hindus to assert that the *śruti* texts should be accepted as Divine authority.[5] He believed that compromise with *Smṛti* texts was the bane of Hindu religious thought and that the most disastrous cause of Hindu degeneration was replacement of the authority of the

Vedas by less authoritative accretions of man-made texts such as the *Mahābhārata* and, more specially, the Purāṇas.[6]

In Swami Dayananda's work, in fact in his entire struggle for a restructuring and rejuvenation of Hindu life and thought, he emphasized his conviction that a total misconception existed in the minds of Hindus concerning the role of scriptural authority. Dayananda's struggle centred around Hindu practices that represented some rather grotesque misconceptions of true religious behaviour. He set about his task of restructuring Hindu thinking by beginning with what he saw as the most glaring theological weaknesses and an obvious failure to assert the position of scripture within a Hindu doctrinal framework.

It is now one of the cardinal principles of the Arya Samaj movement that the authority of the Vedas is accepted without question. This assertion allows no compromise, despite the long-standing view that the *Bhāgavad Gītā* occupied the central position, the very core of Hindu thought in society for many centuries. Dayananda asserted that the Vedas were the supreme authority for all of Hinduism and no other scripture could occupy this position under any circumstances.[7] Commentaries on the Vedas he said were dependent on the Vedas and therefore played a secondary role in scriptural exposition.[8] They were therefore only acceptable if, and only if, they conformed to Vedic teachings and were never a substitute, nor intended as such for Vedic teachings or doctrinal authority.[9]

The Arya Samaj accepted its third principle: viz. "The Vedas are the scriptures of true knowledge. It is the first duty of the Aryan to read them, teach them, recite them and hear them being read"[10] as one of its cardinal doctrines and makes acceptance of it a basic rule for all who wish to be considered members of the Arya Samaj. All Arya Samajists are told of Swami Dayananda's belief that the Vedas are the books of true knowledge, hence it is the paramount duty of every Arya to read them. Swami Dayananda's work, the *Rigvedadi Bhashya Bhumika*, is an introduction to the Vedas, aimed at facilitating Vedic study.

Swami Dayananda's views concerning the Vedas, although reflecting a traditional viewpoint, are also unique. He is, for example, the only teacher to have referred to such works as the Brāhmaṇas, the six Aṅgas, the six Upaṅgas, the four Upavedas, and the eleven hundred and twenty-seven Shakas as commentaries, entirely dependent upon the Saṁhitā portion of the Vedas. Any passages in these works, he asserted, that contradicted the Saṁhitā had to be summarily rejected.[11]

Swami Dayananda's views on the Vedas differ considerably from other interpretations. The special emphasis he gives to aspects of Vedic teachings is rarely encountered in works by scholars better known outside India. Swami Nikhilananda, for example, says that the Vedas treat of two ideas which rational minds are expected to strive to realise.[12] These are material happiness (*abhyudeya*) and the highest good (*nihśreyasa*). Material happiness is obtained through the observance of ethical laws and worldly duties and the propitiation of benevolent duties through the offering of oblations and sacrifices. Gods were always personified forms of cosmic consciousness controlling human life. The highest good is said to transcend the causal law.

Hinduism traces its origin to the composition of the Vedas. The Vedas, as literary works, came into existence during the Vedic period, which historians divide broadly into three parts:

The Age of the Mantra
The Age of the Brāhmaṇas
The Age of the Upaniṣads[13]

The Mantras or hymns are the poetic compositions, the Brāhmaṇas the ritualistic treatises and the Upaniṣads the mystical or, more correctly, philosophical aphorisms.

The division of the collection of writings into their various segments is the work of Vyasa, who attempted a systematic presentation of the collection of hymns that previously constituted the entire work. Vyasa's success in dividing the Vedas into the four famous works called Ṛg Veda, Sāma Veda, Yajur Veda and Atharva Veda, is the first singularly important contribution to the heritage of literary Hinduism. Each of the Vedas was divided into the Mantras and Brāhmaṇas which constituted Jñāna Kāṇḍa. The Karma Kāṇḍa section was always recognised among Hindu scholars for the worth of the Saṁhitās and Brāhmaṇas as poetic compositions and ritualistic treatises. The classification of the Jñāna Kāṇḍa was due to the contemplative and rationalistic bias engendered by the Āranyakas and Upaniṣads. These divisions do not represent any sequence in time, have always existed together as works representative of human inclinations and symbolise craving of the human mind for both religious consolation and material happiness.

Swami Dayananda's belief in the infallible nature of teachings of the Vedas stems from the viewpoint held by Hindu scholars on the kind of scriptural authority they constitute. Swami Prabhavananda says that the Vedas represent Divine and inexpressable Truth itself.[14] For this reason Hindus claim that the Vedas are divine in origin, quite unlike either the Bible or the Korān.

Swami Dayananda says: "The Rgveda, the Yajurveda, the Sāmaveda and the Atharvaveda were produced by the Supreme and perfect Being, Pārabrahman, who possesses the attributes of self-existence, consciousness and bliss, who is omnipotent and universally adored. The meaning is that the four Vedas are revealed by God alone.[15] However, the point of departure arises from the Hindu contention that works of other religions owe their authority to the delivery of a sacred message, God's word, through a prophet or a messenger to the world at large. God's word was then to be accepted on faith by all who hear it. The Vedas on the other hand are said to be *Apauruśeya*, not of human composition, and constitute a Divine Knowledge given by God to all men who strive for it. Swami Nikhilananda, quoting the great Upaniṣadic commentator Sāyanācārya, says that God created the whole universe out of the knowledge of the Vedas.[16] This is to say that Vedic knowledge existed before the creation of mankind. Hence Swami Nikhilananda's contention that the primary meaning of the name Veda is supersensuous wisdom. He says that the secondary reference to the term Veda is to the words in which that knowledge is embodied.[17] Swami Vivekananda says that by the term Vedas, no books are meant. They refer rather to the accumulated treasury of spiritual laws discovered by the ṛṣis of old at various times.[18]

The traditional Hindu view is that the Vedas constitute a religio-philosophical wisdom on the one hand and on the other the utterances in which that wisdom is preserved. The Vedas require no external agency to confirm their authority as scripture.[19] They are themselves the authority, by virtue of their being the knowledge of God or as it is more frequently described "Eternal Truth". This truth is verifiable by any person who aspires to know it through transcendental consciousness.

Swami Dayananda says that the subject-matter of the Vedas may be divided into four classes:[20] These are Vijñāna (philosophy or metaphysics), *Karma* (action in general), *Upāsanā* (Communion with God) and Jñāna (knowledge in general). Of these, Vijñāna takes precedence as it means realization in knowledge of all things, from God down to a blade of grass.[21]

Before commencing a discussion on the subject-matter of the Vedas we consider the views of two former Arya Samaj scholars on the authority of the Vedas.[22] "The Veda is a Śruti and not a Shastra: a Shastra is a text of systematized knowledge with a scientific terminology. The Sruti has the potential of becoming the source of a Shastra but by itself is not the Shastra." They contend, as Dayananda did, that for understanding the nature of the Śruti, the ancient Indian seers evolved a regular system of other scriptures such as the Vedāṅgas.

The Hindus' knowledge of the universe is theoretically circumscribed by the teachings of the Vedas. To the Hindu, creation is beginningless and endless. God, who contains within Himself the seed, the material cause of the universe, brings forth the universe out of Himself, His own Being, and then in due course takes it back again, withdraws it into Himself. This process of creation and dissolution is endless and constitutes eternity which bears witness to a succession of such cycles of creation and dissolution.[23]

As has already been observed, the orthodox Hindu regards the Vedas as his highest written authority. Any subsequent scripture, if it is to be regarded as valid, must be in agreement with them. It may expand them, or develop them, but never contradict them. They are to him as perfect as any document can be because they are expressive of Divine Truth.

Swami Dayananda's study of the Vedas was exhaustive. His work covers an extensive field as he sought always to confirm that they, and only they, form the highest authority on all matters religious and even on many matters secular. Dayananda says that God had ordained that man should acquire duly, "the Dharma preached by me (God) which is justly devoid of bias and partiality and refulgent with truthful characteristics."[24]

His introduction to the commentary on the Vedas gives simple evidence of his enormous enthusiasm for propagating the idea that the Vedas were authoritative texts for the study of subjects such as astronomy, medicine, science, mathematics, shipbuilding, aircraft construction, telegraphy among others. He says, for example, on the art of shipbuilding that, "A man desirous of possessing and enjoying wealth, riches, necessities of life, comforts and victory should fulfil his desires with the help of physical science. By constructing ships of wood, iron, etc., and by using fire and water (for generating steam for propulsion) he may make voyages on the seas backwards and forwards and in this way he may amass wealth."[25]

Dayananda's difficulty with all the other sacred books of Hinduism is the difficulty of a vast number of Hindus who had to face the many criticisms levelled against them. Many of the Purāṇas in particular were regarded by people such as Griswold[26] and others as the crudest and grossest form of literary immaturity, and much heartache accompanies every effort at scriptural study. It was his keen desire therefore that only the purest and best form of literary and religious excellence portrayed in some of the books of Hinduism should be read and regarded as holy scripture and for this reason was adamant that only the Vedas could stand up to close scrutiny. He has, however, been accused of blaspheming against the Śrimad Bhāgavatam.[27]

Dayananda's contribution to the aspect of Hinduism dealing with its literary authority has been substantial. He has succeeded in focusing attention on this aspect of the faith and in so doing many theologians have looked again at the importance of scriptural texts as sources of authority for spiritual knowledge. Revised editions of the Vedas with English translations have since appeared and more people are now taking to Vedic study where previously this was quite uncommon among most Hindus in every country in the world.

REFERENCES

1. Nikhilananda, S., *Vivekananda: The Four Yogas and Other Words*, Ramakrishna Centre, New York, 1953, p. 185.
2. Nikhilananda, S., *Self-Knowledge*, Ramakrishna Mission, Madras, 1967, p. 7.
3. Nikhilananda, S., *Ibid.*, p. 7.
4. Dayananda, S., *Commentary on the Vedas*, Jan Gyan Prakashan, Delhi, 1973.
5. Dayananda, S., *Satyartha Prakash*, Jan Gyan Prakashan, Delhi, 1973. p. 196.
6. Dayananda, S., *Ibid.*, p. 197.
7. Lal, V., *Handbook of the Arya Samaj*, Jan Gyan Prakashan, New Delhi, 1930, p. 35
8. Pareek, R.S., *Arya Samaj in the Making of Modern India*, Rajasthan University of Jaipur, 1975.
9. Pareek, R.S., *Ibid*, p. 98.
10. Pareek, R.S., *Ibid*, p. 99.
11. Dayananda, S., *Satyartha Prakash*, p. 563.
12. Nikhilananda, S., *Self-Knowledge*, p. 9.
13. Sarma, D.S., *Hinduism Through the Ages*.
14. Prabhavananda, S., *Spiritual Heritage of India*, Ramakrishna Math, Madras, 1977.

15. Dayananda, S., *Commentary on the Vedas,* , Jan Gyan Prakashan, New Delhi, 1973.
16. Nikhilananda, S., *Self-Knowledge*, p. 20.
17. Nikhilananda, S., *The Upanishads*, Ramakrishna Centre, New York, 1970, p. 31.
18. Vivekananda, S., *Hinduism*, Ramakrishna Math, Madras, 1960.
19. Dayananda, S., *Satyartha Prakash.*
20. Dayananda, S., *Commentary on the Vedas.*
21. Dayananda, S., *Satyartha Prakash.*
22. Satya Prakash, S., Vidyalankar, S., *Rigveda Samhita*, Veda Pratishthana, New Delhi, 1977, p. 4.
23. Nikhilananda, S., *The Upanishads*, Ramakrishna-Vivekananda Centre, New York, 1977, pp. 64-65.
24. Dayananda, S., *Satyartha Prakash*, p. 60.
25. Dayananda, S., *Satyartha Prakash*, p. 116.
26. Griswold, H.D., *The Religion of the Rigveda*, Motilal Banarsidass, Delhi, 1971.
27. This was a criticism leveled against him by members of the Iskcon, the International Society for Krishna Consciousness in a private interview.

CHAPTER 2

Theory of Divine Revelation

HINDUS BELIEVE that the Vedas are of Divine origin and were revealed to man when he first sought to know Reality. The contents of the Vedas, referred to as Śruti (what is revealed or known), are not subject to human composition (apauruśeya) and reflect an essential message Hindus believe to be the "Eternal Truth". Swami Vivekananda's view best epitomises this statement:

> "The Hindus have received their religion through Revelation: the Vedas. They hold that the Vedas are without beginning or end. By the Vedas are meant the accumulated treasury of spiritual laws discovered by different persons at different times."[1]

Swami Nikhilananda describes them in the following way: "The superconscious experiences of the ancient Hindu seers have been embodied in the Vedas, the sacred scriptures of Hinduism. The Hindus believe that the Vedas, containing truths regarding the soul, the universe and Ultimate Reality, are eternal, without beginning and not ascribable to human authorship. They are co-existent with the Creator and form the very basis of creation. These truths are revealed from time to time to the hearts of men and women purified by the practice of self-control and meditation."[2] He continues that the Vedas deal with timeless truth, and are therefore eternal.[3] Little, if anything, is known about the Ṛṣis to whom these truths were revealed because the truths per se are of greater value to man than the personalities to whom they were revealed.

Swami Dayananda supports the contention that the Vedas were revealed to man by God.[4] Revelation in his teaching is expressed as divine inspiration occurring in the lives of the great Vedic Ṛṣis. His belief is that God imparts His knowledge to man, not through the use of the organ of speech but "has revealed knowledge to the soul by virtue of His being the innermost ruling spirit."[5] For Swami Dayananda revelation hinges on the ideal of "uncovering" from within, which is effected through God's incorporeality and His being present in man. He thus reveals His knowledge from within. This knowledge must be seen as being based in the Vedas wherein the first and original Revelation was effected. All subsequent revelations can only confirm for each man the Divine nature of his own being.

Persons thus illumined with such revelation have the task of imparting their knowledge to others. Such knowledge is a preparation for the whole of revelation to occur in every man. Preparation through other religious disciplines is important, because God reveals the truth to such a man who has performed *tapas*, austerity. Such men are inspired through His being, which is the spirit within every man.[6] God, to reveal His truth, the truth of His existence, needs no organ of speech. His revelation comes in the form of knowledge which enlightens man to the fact of Revelation.

The Vedas, Dayananda says, are the original revelation to man at the beginning of man's life on earth. The knowledge of the Vedas is now a record for man's benefit and instruction. By studying the Vedas man becomes inspired in the way the Ṛṣis were inspired and he thus becomes enlightened. For Truth to be made known to others, where no similar Revelation occurs, man must spread Vedic truth by word of mouth. It was Dayananda's firm belief that the original Revelation occurred at a particular time and place in history.[7] For him verification of such revelation occurs in the logic of reason which affirms not only the possibility of such revelation but its actual occurrence. Vedic Revelation occurring as it did at a particular place and time is not indicative of any limitations set on it. To all men who wish to know the truth, to them will it be made known. Firstly, the necessity of study becomes clear and then Divine Revelation becomes manifest.[8]

Swami Dayananda clung tenaciously to his belief that original Revelation occurred to the Ṛṣis of Vedic times. This confirms that Vedic truth and revelation are "as old as mankind".[9] The antiquity of the Vedas is a factor of their uniqueness. The significance of Dayananda's contribution to Hindu liturgy lies in his contention that Vedic truth is meant for all mankind. The Vedas, he believed, had to be studied by all, irrespective of caste, sex, race or nation.[10]

A difficulty in Dayananda's concept of the fact of revelation is that if a spiritual truth is to be made known, nothing is said of revelation as an occurrence within the mind of man. Unlike the view of the Apocalypse as found in Christian thought, in which some form of "uncovering" or "laying bare" occurs, Dayananda places little if any, emphasis on "enlightenment" or "making known" as might be found with Vedāntic thought, hence the difficulty of understanding precisely the nature of revelation in the life of the common man.

However, one fact becomes abundantly clear in the emphasis that Dayananda placed upon the study and knowledge of Vedic truth. His deepest concern lay in what he saw as the superstition and triviality of religious conception arising as he believed from the study of books such as the Purāṅas, which conveyed no truth or lofty religious conception.

Dayananda's primary intention for the Hindu cause in his country was to rid it of the superstition and malpractice with which it was plagued. In order to do this it was necessary to seek out a new theory and subsequently formulate a methodology of reform. Reform, he argued, lay in the Arya Samaj's ability to restore Hinduism to its original purity and to unite Hindus of every community, caste, sect and even language group into a common Hindu humanity. The divisions that plagued the country were symptomatic of the neglect of divine truths embodied in revealed scripture. His dream lay in uniting his people by infusing in them a sense of religious purpose and this he saw in the proclamation that Vedic Truth was the common heritage of all Hindus, if not all mankind, and for those who could understand he propagated the belief that the revelation of the Vedas was their source of both material and spiritual success.[11]

One of the main principles for his belief in the possibility of uniting Hindus to this objective was the fact that all the great Ăcāryās of Hinduism proclaimed the divinity of the Vedas and inspired towards the realisation of the Eternal Truths they taught. Thus Divine Revelation for Dayananda was not only the spiritual directive for Hindu enlightenment but also the basis for a national socio-political and cultural unity and regeneration.[12]

It was therefore necessary, he believed, to lay the foundation for unity, declaring that God's Revelation lay in the Saṁhitās (the mantra portion of the Vedas) and he saw that condemnation of the Purāṇas formed a corollary to this contention. For Dayananda, Vedic Revelation was the means for the religious salvation of the people of India. It was also the means and the basis for her social, economic and political salvation. He urged people wherever he went to study the Vedas, constantly reminding them that the degeneration one saw everywhere was due to the neglect of study of Holy scripture and that the panacea for all ills in the country lay in the acquisition of a new scientifically orientated education. Scientific knowledge, he asserted, had its roots in the Vedas which contained much information of value to young scientists.[13]

Dayananda's convictions were best expressed when he said that "the eradication of inequities is the end of my life".[14] The Revelation that brought into existence the Vedas is the very revelation that makes possible salvation, "the state of emancipation from the endurance of pain, subjection to birth and death" which lead to "liberty and happiness in the immensity of God".[15]

The concept of revelation presupposes hidden truth. In Hindu law discovery of truth has led teachers to conclude that such discovery is always possible. Not as an accident of fate but as the consequence of disciplined striving. Thus "revelation", for all its technical implications, stands subject to examination through Vedic study which enhances the ideal of making known the presence of God. But revelation in the Upaniṣadic sense extends beyond the realm of mental or sense experience.[16]

The Vedāntic proposition on ultimate experience centres on the contemplative ideal which culminates in a meditative awareness of the revelation between sense experience and inward realisation. For Dayananda revelation was possible for man because God is the "innermost ruling spirit" which makes revelation possible from within man.

Unlike many Catholic or Protestant viewpoints, which affirm that Revelation is the disclosure of supernatural truths not attainable by reason,[17] Dayananda tends to the view that thought and logical reasoning lend support to the ideal of striving after the knowledge God makes possible. The general consensus among Hindus focuses on the metaphysical proposition that revealed knowledge enables man to grasp at a higher truth until knowledge of the Supreme Truth becomes known. Dayananda saw Revelation in terms of social justice or, as Luther expressed it, "as the righteousness of God."[18] Dayananda does not extend the ideal of Revelation as a necessary experience for all. The biblical usage reminds the faithful of their place as "hearers of revelation", meaning that those who bear the words of scripture such as the Old or New Testament shall have revealed to them the goodness and mercy of God. Dayananda's belief in the value of the Vedas may be understood as the plea for the possibility of revelation occurring at any time, for God speaks to man through scripture at all times. Dayananda, however, insists that revelation can occur only to "truly holy persons". It would appear therefore that such revelation, having occurred in Vedic times, does not occur in the same way among the generality of mankind, except under circumstances made possible by man's aspiration to the highest Truth.

Swami Dayananda's acceptance of the theory of revelation is contained in the teaching of the method by which revelation takes place. Revelation for Hindu mystics is usually synonymous with mystic introversion by which Truth and the understanding of it becomes known intuitively. Swami Dayananda agrees that verbalisation of Truth is necessary for the purpose of communication. When that Truth is imparted as in the case of a teacher communicating with a student, the verbalisation of a truth is both possible and necessary. But God's revelation to man takes place because God is able to reveal such knowledge to the soul by virtue of His being present within it, a part of man's innermost being, the very soul which is the innermost part of man. "As God is incorporeal and all-pervading He reveals this whole Vedic knowledge to the souls in virtue of His being within."[19]

Many authorities on Hinduism attempt in their writings to establish the absolute infallibility of the Vedas. Efforts have often been made to establish the exact nature of their authority, arising as it does from the standpoint of their being revealed scriptures as opposed to merely inspired writings. The Arya Samaj movement has no specific doctrine, as far as one is able to determine, on the call to a specific type of religious obedience. Within the Arya Samaj movement no attempt is made to direct the spiritual calling in a way that would lead aspirants towards a doctrinal goal in the same way that movements such as the Ramakrishna Centre make upon students. Clearly, within such a movement specific directions are given by inspired men for spiritual aspiration to be pursued along a path which would lead to revelation. The inspiration enjoyed by the Ṛṣis of old, which culminated in the claims of Revelation, is available to all people who strive after such revelation by observing the rules of religious obedience.

Among the inspired teachers, Patañjali held the view that the words conveying the message of wisdom were not in themselves eternal, but the knowledge or ideas concerning Supreme Truth. Hence the Vedas themselves, while being viewed as inspired words of

God, are in fact the means by which *Sphota*—Supreme Knowledge—is conveyed to man. Thus the Vedas, although carrying inspired words, are in fact carriers of spiritual truths affecting man through revealed or inspired knowledge, in ways unique to each person who strives for such knowledge.

The Vedas were not at first committed to writing. This happened only when the writing form became known, and even then not until some inspired men saw the wisdom of committing them to writing. Most believed the words of the Vedas too sacred to write down. Written words became the property of all, whereas the Vedas were originally meant only to be studied by inspired students studying under the direction of inspired teachers. The Vedas could make no claim to infallible authority because the words as language, used to convey Sphota, are themselves not infallible. The call to spiritual obedience is ever present, because it is inspired by discerning students. But revelation, Supreme Revelation, is reserved only for a select few whose spiritual struggle endows them with the gift of such revelation.

REFERENCES

1. Vivekananda, S., *Hinduism*, Ramakrishna Math, Madras, 1960, p. 6.
2. Nikhilananda, S., *Self-Knowledge*, p. 7.
3. Nikhilananda, S., *Ibid*, p. 7.
4. Dayananda, S., *Commentary on the Vedas*, p. 5.
5. Dayananda, S., *Satyartha Prakash*, p. 196.
6. Dayananda, S., *Ibid*, p. 197.
7. Dayananda, S., *Ibid*, p. 197.
8. Dayananda, S., *Ibid*, p. 198.
9. Lal, V., *Handbook of the Arya Samaj*, p. 35.
10. Dayananda, S., *Satyartha Prakash*, p. 199.
11. Pareek, R.S., *Arya Samaj in the Making of Modern India*, p. 98.
12. Pareek, R.S., *Ibid*, p. 98.
13. Pareek, R.S., *Ibid*, p. 99.
14. Dayananda, S., *Satyartha Prakash*, p. 563.
15. Dayananda, S., *Ibid*, p. 566.
16. *Katha Upanishad*, II, III, 13.
17. Harvey, V., *Dictionary of Christian Theology*.
18. Dayananda, S., *Satyartha Prakash*, p. 196.
19. Dayananda, S., *Satyartha Prakash*, p. 198.

CHAPTER 3

The Concept of God

THE TRADITIONAL APPROACH to the development of a full concept of God as "primary cause of all true knowledge", usually follows a course that traces such development from the earliest beginnings of religious thinking in India to the highest flights of religio-philosophical conceptualisations known. Swami Dayananda's approach circumvents this traditional development. He emphasizes numerous Vedic passages which he claims are clear on their conceptions and descriptions. In exploring what it means to "believe in God", consideration has to be given to the experiences Dayananda had and the serious implications they in turn had for formulating his beliefs and the theoretical conceptualisations that emanated from them. A discussion on Dayananda's investigations resulting in the Arya Samaj's religious phenomenology must be found in his "experiential dimension", as Ninian Smart[1] describes it.

While it may be true that Dayananda's emphasis on Vedic revelations was the basis for his conceptualisations, difficulties arise in reconciling these notions with the Upaniṣadic conceptualisation emphasized by people like Vivekananda and other notable authorities in Hindu thought, particularly Vedāntins. In the Ṛg Veda, for example, a process of sublimation arises both from fear of, and reverence for, nature and the environment. Śri Kṛṣṇa's words, representative of God's in the Bhagavad Gītā, echo a Vedāntic sentiment: "I am the origin of all; from Me all (the whole creation) proceeds. Knowing this, the wise worship Me, endowed with conviction." X, 8.[2]

For the ancient Vedic seers contemplation of nature appears to have been important. This was the initial outpouring of devotion which developed into reverence for things easily seen but not easily understood. Thus the glorious sun, a shining orb that rose each day to eliminate darkness and bring new light and life, became Sūrya, the sun god. The receding darkness produced Varuna, a god of the night. This presence of practical needs, it becomes apparent, produces a commonplace of psychology as Griswold contends.[3] Because primitive man found himself in an environment partly helpful and partly untoward and perilous, his fear of or reverence for such phenomena as rivers, rain, fire and wind would dominate his thought and action. The process of personification led to the development of such votaries as "personal gods" and "special gods".

Swami Dayananda, in acknowledging the existence of "extraordinary properties" in natural things, condoned their objectification as Devatās, having qualities that elevate them to a higher status, never, however, to the same status as God. In answer to the question: "Do you believe that the Veda talks of many Gods?" he emphatically answers: "There is no whisper of it in all the four Vedas."[4] He then continues "it is clearly written that there is but one God." There is a description of many 'devatās' in the Vedas. Anything having luminous properties is called devatā, e.g. the earth, the sun, etc.[5]

The grandeur of nature thus evokes within the early Indian mind poetic conceptualisations of metaphysical Truth; their spiritual temperament coupled with meditative introspection produced a religious consciousness which enabled them to feel that the natural phenomena were expressions of celestial power. The Satapaṭha Brahmana echoes the sentiment expressed in Bṛhadāraṇyaka Upaniṣad III, IX, 1-3. Vivagdha the student asks of Yajnavalkya his teacher, "How many in fact are the gods O, Yajñavalkya?" Each time the question was posed a modified answer was given in descending order, beginning with three thousand and three and three hundred and three to thirty-three, six, three, two, one and a half and one. Vivagdha's question finally prompted Yajnavalkya's more comprehensive response on gods, the Vasus, the Rudras, the Ādityas, fire, earth, the sky, the sun, moon, heaven and stars.[6] They are called Vasus because they enable men to live on earth. Swami Dayananda affirms the traditional answer which accepts that the eight Vasus are the abode of creatures, the eleven Rudras the vital forces within the body, the twelve Ādityas, the signs of the Zodiac and one Prajāpati the lord of creatures, which divides into two, prāna and akāśa (energy and matter).[7] He however contends that the one God is "Lord of all these objects and the greatest of all; the One infinite and Inexpressible Supreme Power." It thus became an article of faith in the Arya Samaj movement not to reject the description of the Sathapaṭha Brahmana but to recognise it as the multifarious description of the One Supreme Being.[8]

The Arya Samaj movement, under Swami Dayananda's direction, has accepted as its First Principle, God as the source of all knowledge:

"God is the primary source of all true knowledge and of all that is known by its means."[9] Arya Samaj commentators refer to this as the Primordial Root, the Eternal Unseen sustainer, the source of all true knowledge and of objects made known by true knowledge. They saw this principle as the first enunciation of a theistic outlook. God, they declare, is the first teacher who inspired the knowledge that man now has as a result of this revelation through the Vedas. His Being is distinct from His creation because he manifests Himself through it, and also because of His caring for and communication with mankind.

The second principle reads: "God is existent, conscious, all beatitude, formless, just, merciful, unbegotten, infinite, unchangeable, beginningless, incomparable, the support of all, the Lord of all, All-pervading, Omniscient and Controller of all from within, ever mature, imperishable, fearless, eternal and Creator of the Universe. To Him alone worship is due."[10]

To God are ascribed the qualities of *Sat*, *Cit*, *Ānanda*, (Existence, Knowledge and Bliss). He thus endows Himself with the gifts that enable Him to participate in love and care for humans and all life on earth in a way no other being can. God is described by Dayananda as incorporeal, one and formless, hence free of the possibility of all iconographic representation or even misrepresentation.[11]

"The Vedas teach the worship of One God who is Omnipresent, Omniscient and Omnipotent Lord of the universe."[12] The Atharva Veda (Mandala X, Chapter XXIII, Mantra 38), says:

> "He who is the most exalted of all, who is worthy of being adored by all, who pervades the entire universe, the Omniscient Being, who supports the firmament, who survives the dissolution of the world into the primary atoms, even he is Brahman."[13]

Among the famous hymns of the Ṛg Veda are the Puruṣa Sūkta and the Hiraṇyagarbha Stotram. The Arya Samaj has selected several stanzas of the Hiraṇyagarbha Stotram for chanting at all ritual ceremonies, because it is accepted that all Arya Samaj ritual is accompanied by the performances of the *havan*. Several of the mantras are selections from the Hiraṇyagarbha Stotram. At least one is taken from the Íśa Upaniṣad, which Swami Dayananda regarded as secondary in importance.[14] The mantra is the eighteenth stanza of the Íśa Upaniṣad and is well-known to all Hindus.

The thirteenth mantra of the first section of Mahānārāyana Upaniṣad reads: "The Self-luminous reality is one without a second and is the Creator of heaven and earth." A stanza more acceptable to Arya Samaj chanting and therefore belief is stanza eighteen:

> "Having pervaded the worlds and the created beings and all the quarters and intermediate quarters, the first-born of Brahman known as Prajāpati or Hiraṇyagarbha became by His own nature Pārabrahman, the ruler and protector of individual souls."[15]

Section One stanza 12 of the Mahānārāyana Upaniṣad reads:

> "The Self-luminous Lord renowned in the scriptures pervades all the quarters of heaven. Having been born as Hiraṇyagarbha in the beginning He indeed is inside the universe represented as the womb. He alone is the manifold world of creation now springing into existence and causing the world of creation yet to come. As one having face everywhere, He dwells also as the innermost self leading all creatures."[16]

These specific stanzas chosen for chanting are selected on the basis of their having no direct reference to God as manifesting this universe from Himself. Hence they do not propound the Vedāntic viewpoint.

Swami Dayananda insisted that the ancient Aryans accepted the oneness of God and that the worship of numerous gods and goddesses was introduced in later times. His struggle was centred against Purāṇic Hinduism so prevalent in his day. His objective was to reinstate the study of the Vedas as basic scripture.[17] Dayananda was of the view that because man is finite and limited he can have no adequate conception of the Divine Spirit, the infinite power behind all thought and life. Because God is all pervading and transcendent, man's reverence for Him has to take account of the fact that direct perception is difficult.

He rejected the doctrine of the personality of God because to him this meant earthly, material limitations. His endeavour was therefore strongly directed at showing that the Vedas condemned idolatry in every form.[18] The monotheistic tradition was thus firmly laid within the Arya Samaj movement but much can be said for this being a purely reactionary phenomenon. Not much can be said for the way monotheism was ultimately substantiated and finally vindicated within the movement.[19]

A strong criticism that is levelled against Swami Dayananda is his seeming inability or refusal to take a more comprehensive view of the conflicting theological positions in India of his day. While students have for long borne witness to the dichotomy of theological stance between the followers of Śaṅkara and the Advaitic school and Rāmānuja and the Viśiṣṭadvaita tradition, many scholars see no conflict between them but viewpoints that merit attention in more ways than one. A true spiritual aspirant in the Hindu tradition has the duty always to reconcile all viewpoints because Truth involves a comprehensive outlook on life.

From this position stems the belief in the validity and truth of all world religions. It is in this respect, however, that Swami Dayananda's position was open to justifiable criticism.

The charge is also laid that if stanzas from the Hiraṇyagarbha Stotram are chosen for chanting, they ought to be selected as a starting point which ultimately could lead to understanding and acceptance of such stanzas, as for example, Katha Upaniṣad: II, iii, 14:[20]

> When all desires clinging to one's heart fall off, then a mortal becomes immortal and one attains Brahman here.

And finally the depth of significance that lies in the śloka of the eighteenth chapter of the Bhagavad Gītā:

> "Through devotion he comes to know Me, what My measure is and who I am in truth; then having known Me in truth, he forthwith enters into Me."[21]

The Muṇḍaka Upaniṣad says in II, ii, 11: "This world is nothing but Brahman."[22] Śaṅkara in his commentary on this Śloka says: "All ideas of non-Brahman are but ignorance like the idea of the snake superimposed on a rope. Brahman alone is the Supreme Truth. This is the declaration of the Vedas."[23]

Swami Dayananda found it difficult to reconcile this passage with the experience of suffering. Upadhyaya says:[24] He believes in a spiritual principle as the basis of the world, which is not treated as an illusion. For while Brahman is eternally free from all imperfection, matter is unconscious and the individual souls are subject to ignorance and suffering. So Dayananda stands diametrically opposed to all suggestions that the Advaita position may find reconciliation in his beliefs. He says emphatically:

> "Three things are eternal, namely God, Soul and Prakṛit—the material cause of the universe. They are also known as eternal substances. Being eternal, their essential qualities, their functions and their natures are eternally the same."[25]

The following oft-quoted Vedic passage is acknowledged by

Swami Dayananda to be most crucial, as it stands as a counter argument to the accusation that Hindus believe in many gods. The Ṛg Veda I, 164, 46 reads: "They call Him Indra, Mitra, Varuna, Agni, and He is heavenly, noble winged Gautman. He is one, sages call Him by many names."

Several other passages contribute to the notion concerning the unity of God as an Infinite Being who is referred to through the many deities described in the Vedas. The sublimity of ideas however have to find culmination in the notion of one Supreme Being. Swami Dayananda accepts the sānkhya tradition by acknowledging dualistic concepts of God and soul. "Both God and Soul are eternal", says Sharda, reiterating Swami Dayananda's acceptance of the twin concepts of God and Soul as separate entities in addition to Prakṛti. Their respective natures he saw as eternal, also having separate attributes.[26]

Two of the most powerful institutions founded in India as a result of the existence of two great teachers are the Arya Samaj and the Ramakrishna movement. They are, however, diametrically opposed in several areas of doctrine. Concerning the concept of God, Dayananda accepts God and Soul as separate entities both having eternal existence. He is also adamant that God is infinite, bodyless and immortal and therefore can never manifest Himself on earth, as the doctrine of the Avatāra submits. This stands in direct contradiction to the statement by Sri Ramakrishna in the form acknowledged by his disciples.[27] Dayananda says "God is immaterial and formless."[28] Had He been material and with definite form another Being would have been necessary to supply Him with the physical qualities He would need to take birth in human form on earth. Dayananda says that "if it be urged that God made His own body himself out of His will and desire, it is replied that it only proves the thesis, that He was immaterial before the formation of His body." Hence, concludes Dayananda, God can never assume human form but instead is the uncaused cause, immaterial and invisible cause of all material objects of the world.

Swami Dayananda's understanding of Vedic philosophy stands in sharp contrast to the Upaniṣadic philosophy interpreted within the Ramakrishna movement. He makes no distinction, for example, between what Nikhilananda refers to as the two-fold access to all knowledge: one lower derived through sense-organs and corroborated by varied evidence based upon sense experience. The other higher knowledge, transcendent and realised through vigorous spiritual discipline.[29]

The subject-matter of Upaniṣadic enquiry is Brahman. As used in the Upaniṣads Brahman is Absolute, transcending time, space, cause, result, not to be comprehended by the human intellect and not to be described in words. The unitive knowledge of religious science in the Hindu tradition is Brahma vidyā, knowledge of Brahman. Swami Dayananda disagrees.[30]

Thus those aspects of philosophical Hinduism which seem to have made a strong impact upon students taking a more enlightened interest in Hindu thought are amenable to discussing, for example, the core of Yajñavalkya's teachings in the Bṛhadāraṇyaka Upaniṣad. "You cannot see that which is the seer of seeing, you cannot hear that which is the hearer of hearing; you cannot think that which is the thinker of thought and you cannot know the knower of knowledge."[31]

Brahman is the term used in Hindu philosophical search for numerous descriptions of the concept of God. The compound term Sat-Cit-Ānanda comes close to acceptance of a determinative conceptual factual ideal. Thus Brahman as the First Principle is a unitive basis pervading the universe and yet remains beyond it. Swami Dayananda's dualistic concept differs radically from this traditionally accepted view. He describes men and animals in the observable world as possessing a reality which cannot be denied. "Souls and nature are not like Brahman; they are inferior to it." He asserts more emphatically: "Therefore, it is proved that Brahman is always one, and the souls and elements existing in nature are many."[32]

Belief in God has often been characterised as primarily involving the cultivation of particular attitudes towards reality, specified by a community of faith, which maintains a set of traditions, rites and practices in which the believer participates. Dayananda's confrontation with two foreign monotheisms, Islam and Christianity, also meant a certain respect for some aspects of their teachings. He noticed that each had a compact and definite creed and concluded that unless Hinduism developed its own, it was only a matter of time before they won the day and annihilated the ancient faith.[33]

Part of what it means to believe in God is participation in rites and ceremonies. This means that even if they don't bring fulfilment in liberation at least they hold to a promise of liberation. It is therefore proper to establish central characteristics on the purpose of religious belief.[34] Dayananda found it necessary to enunciate his belief with the highly emotive calling: "He who is called Brahm the Most high, who is Paramatman or the Spirit, who permeates the whole universe, who is Truth, Intelligence and Happiness; whose nature, attributes and doings are holy, who is omniscient, incorporeal, all pervading, unborn, infinite, almighty, just and merciful; who is the author of the universe; its protector and destroyer, who weighs the merits and demerits of individuals according to requirements of absolute justice, Him, I believe to be the Lord of Creation."[35]

REFERENCES

1. Smart, N., *The Concept of Worship*, MacMillan, London, 1972.
2. Radhakrishnan, S., *The Bhagavad Gita*, George Allen and Unwin, London, 1956.
3. Griswold, H.D., *The Religion of the Ṛg Veda*, Oxford University Press, 19 p. 81.
4. Dayananda, S., *Satyartha Prakash*, p. 112.
5. Vedalankar, N., *Shastra Navanitam*, Veda Niketan, Durban, 1982, p. 473.
6. Madhavananda, S., *The Brhadāraṇyaka Upanishad*, Advaita Ashrama, Calcutta, 1965.
7. Dayananda, S., *Ibid*, p. 173.
8. Dayananda, S., *Ibid*, p. 178.
9. Shastri, V., *The Arya Samaj: Its Cult and Creed*, Arya Pratinidhi Sabha, Delhi, 1967.
10. Shastri, V., *Ibid*, p. 150.
11. Dayananda, S., *Ibid*, p. 176.
12. Pandit, S.S., *Arya Samaj Contribution to Education*, University of Baroda, Baroda, 1974.
13. Dayananda, S., *Rig Veda—Vol. 1*, Tr Vidya Martanda, Sarvadeshik Arya Pratinidhi Sabha, Delhi, 1974.
14. *Arya Prayer*, Veda Niketan, Durban, 1981.
15. Vimalananda, S., *Mahanarayana Upanishad*, Ramakrishna Math, Madras, 1979, p. 25.
16. Mal, Bahadur, *Dayananda: A Study in Hinduism*, Sarvadeshik Arya Pratinidhi Sabha, Delhi, 1967. p. 104
17. Lillington, Frank, *The Brahma Samaj and Arya Samaj in their Bearing Upon Christianity*, MacMillan and Company, London, 1901.
18. Jones, K.W., *Arya Dharma*, Munshiram Manoharlal, Delhi, 1976.
19. Gambhirananda, S., *Eight Upanishads*, Vol. 1, Advaita Ashrama, Calcutta, 1965.
20. Radhakrishnan, S., *The Bhagavad Gita* (XVIII, 55), George Allen and Unwin, London, 1956.
21. Gambhirananda, S., *Eight Upanishads*, Vol. 2, Advaita Ashrama, Calcutta, 1965.
22. Gambhirananda, S., *Ibid*, p. 142.
23. Upadhyaya, G.P., *Philosophy of Dayanand*, Arya Samaj Allahabad, 1955, p. 110

24. Upadhyaya, G.P., *Ibid*, p. 115.
25. Upadhyaya, G.P., *Ibid*, p. 120.
26. Nikhilananda, S., *The Gospel of Sri Ramakrishna*, Ramakrishna Centre, New York, 1977.
27. Dayananda, S., *Satyartha Prakash*, p. 520.
28. Nikhilananda, S., *The Upanishads*.
29. Dayananda, S., *Satyartha Prakash*.
30. Madhavananda, S., *Brhadaranyaka Upanishad*, Advaita Ashrama, Calcutta, 1970.
31. Dayananda, S., *Ibid*.
32. Dayananda, S., *Ibid*.
33. Dayananda, S., *Ibid*.
34. Dayananda, S., *Ibid*.
35. Dayananda, S., *Ibid*.

CHAPTER 4

Concept of Man, Caste and Social Values

IT WAS for Swami Dayananda, as it was for his better known contemporary Swami Vivekananda, a matter of very deep concern that there should develop in India a reorientation in thinking on the social values that dominated Indian society for many centuries. No social values however were worth following, Dayananda concluded, if they were not rooted in Vedic religiosity. Roman Rolland says of him: "Dayananda transformed into the languid body of India his own formidable energy, his certainty, his lion's blood. He reminded the secular passivity of a people, too prone to bow to fate, that the soul is free and that action is the generator of destiny."[1] For a man like Dayananda Indian social values, as they were understood by a vast number of illiterate people, had to undergo drastic overhaul from its very roots. The fundamental problems, he believed, lay in the age-old beliefs and practices which the vast majority of people accepted with almost unthinking inheritance. In his travels Dayananda witnessed aspects of religious practice which raised his scorn, and above all his deep-rooted commitment to institute drastic changes.

Quite clearly the most horrendous features of Indian life were abundantly evident in the iniquitous caste system. For a total change to be effected in this, Dayananda concluded that the very root of the problem lay in the almost incalculable misunderstanding that existed in the minds of the people about religious values and the social system they engendered. For a drastic change to be effected there was need firstly to return to a better understanding of the true law of God as embodied in the true scriptures of India, and from there to nobleness in every man who followed the principles of truth and justice.

For Dayananda, man was a part of creation. And creation was, "That which results from a combination of primary elements compounded together consistently with a thorough and complete knowledge of the distinctive properties of every separate element and with all the perfection of design in all its infinite variety."[2] Creation for him was an entity possessed of eternal existence. Its roots were found in Prakṛti, the material cause of the universe which existed for the purpose of assisting the soul in its onward march to enlightenment. For Dayananda man is a Soul possessed of eternal quality and together the three external substances, God, Soul and matter, acted in combination for mutual benefit.

Dayananda believed that creative energy, sometimes analogous to a play in its manifest form, was the natural exercise of the energy of God. God expresses Himself in His creative energy. The purpose of creation was the essential expression of God's creative energy. And creation had one fundamental purpose apart from its own manifest creativity. This was to provide the field whereby Souls could enjoy action and the fruits of that action. Souls, Dayananda believed, are tied to creation through ignorance. Thus man is a part of creation because as a man he is subject to ignorance and action. But action may be purposeful or it may not be so. The only distinct form of action that bears consideration is purposeful action by which man frees himself from the bonds of ignorance and ultimately attains salvation. Purposeless action is action that perpetuates bondage and bondage is subjugation to eternal creation.[3]

Man is led through ignorance to worship things other than the Creator and obscures his intellectual faculties from which pain and suffering result. Ignorance is termed bondage as it involves man, or more correctly the Soul of man, in pain which man by natural instinct wishes to escape. It is however his lot to suffer pain. And pain is the catalyst necessary for salvation. The emancipation of the soul from pain and suffering of every description, its enjoyment unleashed by the gross physical body to produce a career of freedom in the all-pervading God and His immense creation for a stated period and its resumption of earthly life after the expiration of that period is termed Salvation.[4]

The means of salvation are worship of God and contemplation of His nature and attributes with concentrated attention, the practice of virtue, a thorough control over the passions during the period of study, association with the wise and learned, love of true knowledge, purity of thought and active benevolence. Man is allowed to acquire wealth (*artha*). This is a cardinal principle that says man is entitled to enjoy wealth attained by honesty and fair dealings. Kāma or enjoyment of sense pleasure is possible as it enables man to experience true pleasure through uprightness and honesty.

Dayananda maintains a very strict dualistic position, asserting that those who believe in non-duality "sleep on the rosy bed of ignorance", because "the soul is finite and limited in knowledge" while the supreme Being is infinite, all-pervading and omniscient."[5] Dayananda holds the view that birth, death and suffering are characteristics of the soul, hence God and man are fundamentally separate beings. Ignorance appears in the teachings of Dayananda as fundamental to man's own understanding of himself, so if emancipation is to come it has to be through the elimination of ignorance in which man finds himself. The soul is, however, free to act in the performance of its duties, subject only to the laws of God.[6]

However, while it is in the power of God to create the world, preserve it and if necessary destroy it, while yet maintaining it through natural law, man is not a duplicate creator. Being separate from God, he follows a law different from that of God. As man he propagates his own species and maintains a duty and a responsibility to offspring. He is subject to laws either good or evil. Man's will is therefore subject to desire. Man is distinct from God by the nature of his own qualities, e.g. pain, emotion, pleasure, joy, sadness, knowledge, etc. Man is a soul bent on a specific course of development and so long as the soul of man inhabits a body, so long will man's duties be directed to discovering the laws of God and manifesting the light of the soul.[7]

This manifestation begins with moral, ethical and spiritual discipline. In his views on education Dayananda prescribes rules of behaviour for young people which he extends to adults who follow a strictly religious life.[8]

The religious disciplines he advocates are seen in the light of his contention that "God pervades the soul." For this reason it is possible for man to develop qualities of nobleness because his relationship with God is enhanced by the fact that this relationship is extended by God's "adoration" and love which establishes bonds similar to those between a father and son or master and servant. Thus a union, a kind of similarity, that culminates in fellowship between man and God is established. Similarity between them is marked by *Sādharmya*, (similar qualities) and *anvyabhāva* (necessary connection) that does not imply the advaitic union, but a condition that perpetuates unity while yet maintaining a clear distinction and separateness. God's presence is marked by ubiquity and man's presence by finite limitations.[9]

Man's role in life is to observe and obey God's commandments, which involve avoiding all forms of irreligious behaviour, and to follow devotion to Him through discipline and introspection, following the rules of righteousness and justice. These will ultimately lead to salvation which means, "Living in God, Being in God, maintaining individuality while yet being pervaded by Him."[10]

All mankind belonged in the beginning to one caste. Afterwards, according to the Ṛg Veda and Atharva Veda, man was divided into Aryas or noble people and anaryas or ignorant people. Noble and virtuous people were called Aryas, the learned were devas. The rest were ignorant, low, vicious.[11] A later division occurred which brought into existence from among Aryas themselves a fourfold classification of Brāhmaṇas, Kṣatriyas, Vaiśyas and Śūdras. The caste structure became in the course of time a degenerate system. It had begun with some men struggling hard to attain the qualities of nobility as is proved by Aryavrata enjoying prosperity and progress through the birth of sages, philosophers, princes, emperors.[12] It was inevitable that a form of rigidity in caste would result and the ultimate fossilised condition of the whole caste system would degenerate into an obnoxious social order.

However, Dayananda believed that a Brahmin child is a Brahmin child because his parents are Brahmins. But nothing prevents non-Brahmins from becoming Brahmins, as is clearly illustrated in the Candogya Upaniṣad, which cites the example of Jabala, of unknown parentage, attaining to Brahminhood. Or as the Mahābhārata points out that Visvamitra was regarded as a Brahmin despite his Kṣatriya heritage, and Matanga was first a Caṇḍāla[13] then a Brahmin. Caste merit becomes the cornerstone of Dayananda's philosophy concerning the social order of India. Only he deserves to be a Brahmin, says Dayananda, who has acquired the best knowledge and character while an ignorant person is fit to be a Śūdra. A Brahmin is not classified according to genetic inheritance but by his acts of righteousness.[14]

Dayananda believed that man in society had many duties to perform. These fell into four orders. In essence, priests were men of prayer—those who kept the body clean, purified the will by the practice of truth, the vital spirit by knowledge and devotion through study of philosophy. Those who thus wished to be regarded as Brahmins had to follow no less than fifteen categories of duties ranging from study and practice to faith and belief in the Vedas, God and Salvation. The duties of a Kṣatriya are listed under eleven categories, ranging from protection of people to respect for all. These duties Dayananda extracted from the laws of Manu and the Bhagavad Gītā as well as from the Vedas. The duties of merchants or Vaiśyas were to care for the poor and by means of their acumen to bring prosperity to the land by careful investment. The only duty of a Śūdra was to be of service while shunning slander, envy, pride and all other evil habits.[15]

For Swami Dayananda the distinction between men, as outlined by the caste concept, is made partly by God. Hence a distinction between one and another is part of natural law.[16]

Just as a man is distinguished from birds and animals so too are some men distinguished from others by virtue of their character, their thoughts and meritorious deeds. They are thus also concerned through many other considerations such as the food they eat, the clothes they wear and the company they keep. Thus all men have the right to aim at achieving the noblest standards of behaviour from which would emanate their achieving noble characters. All men achieve nobility by studying the Vedas and attaining to the heights of the spiritual glory they exemplify.[17]

Men of all castes suffer the same pains and enjoy the same delights. Great men have great cares and common people have little anxiety. But all men are subject to the same laws that determine how joy, sorrow, pain and suffering may be experienced. It is a just God who gives to all men their just deserts. It is therefore right to believe that the present life and all existing circumstances are in perfect accord with the consequences of the deeds done in previous lives, and the future will be regulated by the consequences done in the present life.

However, Dayananda continues, "if you compare the pleasure and pain of the world, happiness many times exceeds pain and many pure souls earn the bliss of salvation by constant practice of virtuous actions."[18] All pain has a benign purpose behind it. Swami Dayananda believed that man's life is rooted in Truth, hence by following rules such as the laws of Manu his ethical principles enable him to transcend the laws of caste and attain to the height of righteousness that is steeped in goodness. God is all that is good, for Goodness is equivalent to God. God is the ideal embodiment of Truth, mercy, kindness, justice and perfect morality. He is the ethical ideal.[19]

The roots of a good society lie in the training and ethics afforded to its young people. The young should grow into respectable men and women with profound knowledge of religious values. Religious values direct men in social values and only social values embellished by the virtues of Vedic culture could have any purpose for India and the Indian people.

Hinduism has always taught that the four Puruṣārthas are the ideal goals of life for all Hindus. Swami Dayananda's belief was that *artha* and *kāma* are legitimate desires circumscribed by ethical considerations. He says, however, that wealth is something earned with honesty, justice and fair dealing. Therefore *kāma* or true enjoyment is that which combines the fruit of uprightness of principle and honestly acquired wealth. Add these to the age-old system of caste and we have a model for all people in their recognition of the need for striving for the highest merits of behaviour which enable them to reach the highest caste.

Thus for Dayananda, the strong emphasis he laid on ethics was proof of his determination to stamp out the corruption which featured so strongly in Indian life. Upadhyaya[20] contends that ethics deals with the actions of man and found that Dayananda's ethics were a protest against many prevailing notions of society. He believes that Dayananda was opposed to several of the notions held by rationalist philosophers and even pragmatists, but contends that Dayananda's views echo similarities in the work of William James.

Dayananda believed strongly in the freedom of choice of the individual in his social responsibilities. It was therefore necessary to account for the implications of the doctrine of *kāma*. Radhakrishnan says[21] that the demand for freedom must reckon with a universe that is marked by order and regularity. Past *karma* enables us to live and work within the confines of conditioned actions as they are responses to *Kārmic* law. But freedom of choice in every action enables us to live within the confines of free will while yet being allowed to conduct action as moral and spiritual law dictates. So if social action is to meet standards we consider religiously beneficial we have to live religiously. In the light of those needs of society, its moral integrity and above all the possibilities of building a society enjoying the highest goodness, we become individually strong within religious reckoning.

For this reason, Dayananda finds that the starting point of all action, including social action, is man. Society, he contends, is a collection of individual units and not, as others might contend, an organic whole. Thus he places a vast responsibility on individual action. He therefore contends[22] that the excellence of royalty is derived from the honesty of intentions, the superiority of qualities, the justice of action, freedom from partiality, the maintenance of morality within social order, paternal affection for subjects and perseverance in satisfying their needs and striving for genuine improvement.

It is clear that Dayananda's deep concern for the social regeneration of Indian society had its roots in his seeing many pernicious practices in his country. He found the country broken by castes and could not reconcile this system of social behaviour with many of the notions, in fact the fundamental assertions, concerning the religious life of man as found in the Vedas. It therefore became a focal point of his teachings to abolish many of the social practices of his people. His efforts at reforming Hindu society took into account all the social practices he saw in India. He instituted into the Arya Samaj movement reforms of some practices. Among them were ritual ceremonies such as *Śrādha.* This ceremony was conceived as a compulsory ritual to ensure the salvation of the deceased. He saw no logic in the practice and even less in its belief. This particular ceremony gave rise to a subsequent practice which called for caste dinners in memory of the dead. Needless to say, he ruthlessly condemned the enormous expense, time and effort necessary for a practice that had no religious basis, and called for its removal. He also called for the abolition of child marriages and advocated the removal of the ban on widow marriage. He called for the removal of the obnoxious dowry system, the barter system in a girl's marriage and also the status of perpetual dependency and inferiority accorded to women.[23]

While it was true that Swami Dayananda made outstanding contributions to the regeneration of Hindu society by calling for a removal of many social practices he saw as evil because they had no Vedic basis or authority, it was the *Śuddhī* practice with which he was most deeply concerned. He therefore advocated the starting of a campaign to institute a movement of change. Only a short while after he advocated this practice thirty-five people who had been converted to Islam were reconverted to Hinduism in a formal ceremony that Dayananda conceived and advocated.This was later followed by the reconversion to Hinduism of Hindus who had been converted to Christianity.[24]

Dayananda worked tirelessly in many areas of social reform. His preaching against many of the pernicious practices made the Indian government become aware of the need for reforms. It is in the area of social life that Dayananda's contribution to the reform of Hindu society was recognised and many Acts of Parliament helped to stem the decay that was so evident during his childhood.[25]

REFERENCES

1. Rolland, R., *The Life of Ramakrishna*, Advaita Ashrama, Calcutta, 1970, p. 137.
2. This was the eighth one of the fifty principles that formed Dayananda's basic beliefs.
3. Singh, B.C., *Life and Teachings of Dayananda*, p. 104.
4. The seventh principle.
5. Dayananda, S., *Satyartha Prakash*, p. 132.
6. Dayananda, S., *Satyartha Prakash*, p. 185.
7. Dayananda, S., *Ibid*, p. 187.
8. Dayananda, S., *Ibid*, p. 55.
9. *Ibid*, p. 194.
10. *Ibid*, p. 232.
11. *Ibid*, p. 219.
12. *Ibid*, p. 83.
13. *Ibid*, p. 63.
14. *Ibid*, p. 84.
15. *Ibid*, p. 89.
16. *Ibid*, p. 379.
17. *Ibid*, p. 334.
18. Satyaprakash, S., *Dayananda's Outline of Vedic Philosophy*, Dayananda Sansthan, Delhi, 1975, p. 201.
19. Satyaprakash, S., *Ibid*, p. 216.
20. Upadhyaya, G.P., *Philosophy of Dayananda*, Gyan Mandir, Allahabad, 1955, p. 394.
21. Radhakrishnan, S., *A Hindu View of Life*, George Allen and Unwin, London, 1956.
22. Satyaprakash, S., *Dayananda's Vedic Philosophy*, Dayanand Sansthan, Delhi, 1975, p. 221.
23. Pandit, K.S., *A Critical Study of Arya Samaj Education*, University of Baroda, Baroda, 1974, p. 33.
24. Vidyalankar, Bhimsen, *Arya Pratinidhi Sabha*, Arya Pratinidhi Sabha, Punjab, 1940, p. 311.
25. Pareek, R.S., *Ibid*, p. 161.

CHAPTER 5

Concept of Purpose and Goal of Life

SWAMI DAYANANDA founded the Arya Samaj movement to resuscitate and rejuvenate his people's knowledge of the Vedic gospel. When he separated from his guru, Swami Virjananda, he left with the promise that he would consecrate his life to the annihilation of the many heresies that had crept into the Vedic faith, but above all, "to disseminate the truth."[1] The founding of the Arya Samaj was in a sense a response to the promise made by Dayananda to his guru to re-establish Vedic truth in India. For Vedic Truth, a study of it, practice of it and above all an understanding of it was the single spurt necessary for the re-establishment of righteousness and religious endeavour in the land. The founding of the Arya Samaj was aimed at re-establishing in the minds of all noble people what the true purpose and goal of life was.

Vaidyanath Shastri says, "Here it can be also unequivocally said that the aim of the human quest is to clear out and express the mystery of life and existence."[2] He believed that the "Will and Wisdom of the Creator prevails everywhere in the Universe and the human consciousness has the task of penetrating the mystery of these two experiences."[3]

For Swami Dayananda all people are born into worldly bondage and have to experience misery and pain. However, all of life is not characterised by pain. For both God and the soul are intelligences. The nature of man is holy, immortal and righteous.[4] God, however, has the task of creating, preserving and destroying the world, keeping all things in their respective spheres and subjecting them to laws, reward and punishment.

But for man the enigma of life is still one of his primary concerns. All of human life is irrevocably interrelated with his religious life. The enigma arises from the experience of pain and from it he wishes to experience God which he is led to believe is the fountain-head of bliss. Indian life has always been filled with belief that God is *ānanda*, bliss. The soul in its nature is pure and endowed with consciousness and is immortal. These characteristics and qualities it shares with God. It is, however, ignorance that binds the soul to the mortal body. This ignorance is not of a permanent nature and can be removed if man takes the trouble to do so It has free will which, when exercised, could give it an understanding of how it may be freed of its encumbrances. This involves the soul in a cycle of growth leading to birth, death and rebirth.

For Gautama the Buddha, life was characterised by pain. For Patañjali life was characterised by five kinds of pain. In his Yoga sūtras he refers to them as *avidyā* (nescience), *asmitā* (egotism), *rāga* (attachment), *dveṣa* (aversion) and *abhiniveṣa* (clinging to life). These five causes of pain are the real causes of suffering because they arise from ignorance about their specific purpose. Man's inability to recognise them in their entirety is cause for pain of various kinds. Pain is also mixed with pleasure because many pleasurable experiences are known to end in pain. Sometimes outstanding sportsmen are paralysed in accidents or brilliant students are robbed of life at the moment they embark on careers. Man's experience of pain arises from a wide variety of sources.

Indian philosophy searches out and presents the best possible explanations for the experience of pain. Suffering may have a value or purpose, for only the experience of it can lead to its ultimate transcendence. For philosophy, *ānanda* or absolute bliss is projected as not only a goal but a supreme end where man becomes the enjoyer or experiencer of it. But absolute bliss is only experienced when pain is transcended.

Swami Dayananda, however, qualifies the experience of pain by all men. He is of the view, unlike the Buddha, that all of life is not characterised by pain. He regards life as being subject to pain in only limited spheres. He says in *Satyartha Prakash* that if the pain and suffering of the world can be compared with the amount of pleasure found in it, the experience of pleasure may be seen to exceed it in great measure.[5] He extends this to include the ideals of Truth and Righteousness, and divergence from these eternal and inherent gifts of God he regards as temporary. Man is by nature Truthful because he is born of Truth; he is more righteous by nature and has the fortune also at most times of his life to experience joy and pleasure.

Thus pain and suffering are temporary though very necessary experiences. In fact both pleasure and pain are a fundamental part of the purpose of existence for it is with these that man learns his greatest lessons on their purpose. The purpose behind both pleasure and pain is the same. They are not the direct outcome of one's actions in the same way that cause is related to effect. Pleasure and pain are the result of action aimed at the experience of the one while avoiding the other.

For Dayananda life is filled with the hope of freedom from suffering because it has been created by a Righteous Being. He sees the righteous Being as one grounded in Truth. Hence it became a fundamental principle that all Arya Samajists ought to adhere to Truth and give up untruth. "That person is just who on due consideration adopts truth and relinquishes falsehood, protects the just and expels the unjust."[6]

Life itself sometimes calls on people to undergo intense religious struggle. All men are not similarly called and usually follow interests best suited to their specific temperaments. Thus those who join the *gṛhastha āśrama* or householder's station in life are expected to fulfil other interests such as accumulation of wealth, knowledge, strength and honour in society. The harmonious development of the physical body leads to mental equipoise and the opportunity to work for one's own improvement and the betterment of one's fellow beings in many walks of life. For those who wish to follow a life of intense religious struggle such wishes are granted. All that life demands is that they must be rooted in righteousness and truth. Such an adherence makes for the spiritual advancement we all seek. Thus for Dayananda spiritual growth does not necessarily imply adherence to a life of asceticism. Asceticism for him is equal in value to a householder's life, for each is equally noble. Dayananda, unlike his contemporary Vivekananda, regarded *gṛhastha āśrama* as the highest station in life,[7] because it is during such a period of life that worldly tests are greatest and man experiences his greatest pain in such tests. The life of a renunciant is considerably easier because he confines himself to a limited sphere of worldly intercourse and so limits his exposure to worldly ways and possible suffering.

Either way, a man commits himself to a life of duty and duty for Dayananda is duty towards one's fellow beings. The sixth principle of the Arya Samaj reads:

> "The prime object of Arya Samaj is to do good to the world. That is, to ameliorate suffering in the physical, spiritual and social conditions of all men."[8]

and the ninth principle reads:

> "No one should remain contented with his own well-being but on the contrary, he should regard his well-being as lying in the well-being of others."[8]

In the tenth principle the Arya Samaj accepts that the well-being of society is of greater importance than the well-being of one person.

The altruistic goals that the Arya Samaj sets itself obviously stem from the teachings of Swami Dayananda. He believes that "the purpose of creation is the manifestation of the creative attribute, function and nature of God."[9] God's creative power is recognised by His creating the universe for the purpose of man's salvation. His universe, however, exists in accordance with the perfect design He introduced into His creation. His creation implies the cause of bondage for individual souls. His creation is the subtraction of ignorance and release from such ignorance is the highest goal for man. *Prārthanā* or prayer is an act of soliciting God for the grant of that which may be attained in communion with God.[10]

It stands to Dayananda's credit that the ideal of such striving has been carried through to the upper echelons of society. The inner character of man is his realisation of his ability to attain to the highest perfection which Dayananda advocates. He states: "A state flourishes only as long as men are righteous. It perishes when men fall into vice."[11] The character of a nation is often tied to the character of its government. Governments are sometimes a reflection of the goals and achievements of the people they govern.

Swami Dayananda believes that the goal of life is the attainment of salvation. Salvation he says is release from pain and emancipation from bondage.[12] Bondage is due to ignorance.[13] Man is born into this world to experience suffering. His ignorance of his own duties, both secular and religious, is the cause of suffering but as soon as he realises the need for communion and the proper way to enter into it, he gains the means of earning his salvation and emancipation from bondage. Salvation means earning a place in God, entering into God, being a part of God. This state of being in God is a state of blessedness which lasts for a fixed period of time, before birth in the world is again effected.

The means of salvation are: communion with God through the practice of Yoga; strict observance of religious principles; the attainment of the knowledge of God through study; associating with learned men and ardent perseverance in righteous conduct.[14] In fact, the means of salvation lie principally in obedience to God's commandments and the observance of all moral and ethical rules. These extend to careful living which involves justice, detachment, righteousness and advancement in knowledge irrespective of one's station or situation in life.[15]

Swami Dayananda says that the soul possesses certain senses of its own. So after release the soul develops the ability or power to subsist of its own accord while yet being in God. "Just as the soul does its duties in the world by means of the organs and senses fixed in the body, so does it enjoy happiness of all kinds by means of the powers in the beatific state."[16] Swami Satya Prakash contends that just as it is possible for the soul of man to attain to a state of purity, hence not in perpetual bondage, so it is possible for a soul not to stay perpetually in a state of emancipation. It could return to the earth to take on impurity again and so work towards salvation. The soul has an innate power to do anything it pleases. Its power, however, can be divided into a great variety of aspects such as strength, energy, motion, etc.

The important feature of salvation, unlike the interpretation given to it by Vedāntins, is not dissolution. If dissolution was the effect of true emancipation, the questions arise: "How can such emancipation be appreciated? How does the happiness of such salvation come about? Who is the experiencer of such salvation?" The true effect of salvation for Dayananda lies in release from pain and the happy dwelling in the blissful, all-pervading and Infinite God.[17]

According to Dayananda, this is the view of the Vedānta Sūtras. It is very clearly stated, he says, in the fourth chapter that the soul, when emancipated, lives in Brahman and enjoys all bliss. This interpretation of the Brahma Sūtras by Dayananda is quite unusual, as the Brahma Sūtras are generally regarded as the standard scriptural texts for Vedānta philosophy. The interpretation of this section, however, is not in agreement with that of Śaṅkara who clearly illustrates in his *Adhyasa Bhashya* why such an interpretation cannot be accepted.

Swami Dayananda's interpretation of the rules of release is sometimes described as closely following the notion of release found in Rāmānuja's work. But Cāndogya Upanisad says, "Verily pleasure and pain do not touch one who is bodiless."[18] (VII, xii, I). This clearly illustrates the difference of opinion held on the natures of release, as qualities such as pain, joy, bliss and love are known to man endowed with the mental power of perception of such qualities. The soul of man in a state of release is transcendent and beyond descriptive scrutiny.

Release for the soul is emancipation. Although Swami Dayananda accepts that reincarnation is a fact of life he draws a distinction between emancipation and reincarnation, by which he implies that a soul has yet to gain release. But a soul that gains release can also reassume a body to continue its sojourn on earth. Yet another school of Indian thought asserts that the emancipated soul may also be born as a *jivanmukta* or a soul embodied without being in bondage. Yet another group of thinkers suggests that a cycle of death and life is possible wherein bondage and emancipation characterise its existence. Thus between two bondages there is emancipation. Beyond two emancipations there is bondage. Dayananda, it would appear, accepts this concept of release as being feasible.[19]

Whatever the interpretation it is clear that the idea of eternity has consensus. All emancipation or bondage must be seen as occurring in cycles. For cycles of release and bondage have occurred for all eternity and no explanation could possibly replace this.

On the question of release for the soul, several interpretations have been propounded by various teachers. Swami Dayananda has made his position clear in accepting that bondage is followed by emancipation and emancipation is possible only through struggle while in the embodied state. Whatever views may be expressed on the final state of release, Dayananda enables us to conclude that the experience of life is apparently a limited one because the mind cannot experience all of the soul's series of experiences at one time. We have to conclude that ours is a continuous and everlasting life—a life or lives known only to God who best determines what each soul shall ultimately experience as part of His scheme for His creation in the fulfilment of His will.

Students in the Arya Samaj movement in South Africa have not had any serious difficulty with any of the views expressed by Swami Dayananda on matters of direct theological importance. In general, followers within the movement accept his teachings as a matter of doctrine and seldom enter into any debates or discussion on their implications for Arya Samaj and Hinduism generally. There also appears at times to be a lack of enthusiasm for disseminating these ideas because of the failure of the organisation to provide a basic infrastructure for the dissemination of these theological truths at higher academic level.

Followers of the Arya Samaj doctrines are bound to a course of theological development which will for the foreseeable future be confined to religious services and occasional meetings convened in the presence of visitors from abroad who preach the Arya Samaj doctrine. With the growth of the Ramakrishna Centre and other organisations such as the Divine Life Society, the Society for Krishna Consciousness, the Sai Baba movement and the Śaiva Siddhānta Sangum, South Africa's Hindu community is remiss in not making available facilities for serious discussion on matters of profound theological value.

Within the context of the Arya Samaj movement itself, this shortcoming is particularly evident among young people who have seldom pursued Arya Samaj doctrine beyond the level of simple tracts or the occasional talk or lecture by a local pundit. This is emphasised by the non-availability of suitable books. So far, the Veda Niketan, responsible for publishing works of importance, has failed to provide the movement in this country with any work of profound theological importance. The works of Paṇḍiṭ Nardev remain influential and important, but there is no demand for other works either from Hindus generally or Arya Samajists in particular.

REFERENCES

1. Rolland, R., *Ibid*, p. 132.
2. Shastri, V., *Ibid*, p. 83.
3. Dayananda, S., *Satyartha Prakash*, p. 186.
4. Prabhavananda, S., and Isherwood, C., *How to Know God*, New American Library, New York, 1953.
5. Dayananda, S., *Satyartha Prakash*, p. 207.
6. Dayananda's Beliefs: Belief number nineteen.
7. Dayananda, S., *Satyartha Prakash*, p. 203.
8. Shastri, V., *The Arya Samaj: Its Cult and Creed*, Sarvadeshik Sabha, Delhi, 1967, p. 19.
9. Shastri, V., *Ibid*, p. 62, Belief number nine.
10. Shastri, V., *Ibid*, p. 62, Belief number fifty.
11. Upadhyaya, G.P., *Ibid*, p. 464.
12. Shastri, V., *Ibid*, p. 63, Belief number twelve.
13. Shastri, V., *Ibid*, p. 63, Belief number eleven.
14. Dayananda, S., *Commentary on the Vedas*, Jan Gyan Prakashan, Delhi, 1973.
15. Dayananda, S., *Satyartha Prakash*, p. 232.
16. Dayananda, S., *Satyartha Prakash*, p. 233.
17. Dayananda, S., *Satyartha Prakash*, p. 246.
18. Radhakrishnan, S., *The Principal Upanishads*, George Allen and Unwin, London, 1956.
19. Satya Prakash, S., *Outline of Vedic Philosophy*, Dayananda Sansthan, Delhi, 1975, p. 196.

SECTION FIVE

AFFILIATED INSTITUTIONS

Introduction

THE PROGRAMMES of religious, educational and social upliftment initiated by people like Swami Vivekananda and Swami Dayananda had had very far reaching repercussions in India. These have formed a new structural-functional base for the religious action systems introduced by either teacher and their messages of reform have been received with almost euphoric appreciation among those familiar with the two movements. In a previous chapter it was stated that Swami Dayananda's deep concern for Hindu society was the most important motive for his initiation of a number of social and educational facilities in various parts of the country. The life and message of Swami Dayananda clearly infuse strength into the whole range of Arya Samaj teachings, and have initiated a vigorous renaissance within Hinduism.

Seen culturally, religion is part of the complex of prescriptions and proscriptions that guides the interactions of men in society. Dayananda understood these prescriptions as rooted in the speaking of Truth. Also, all acts of virtue were consistent with the commandment of God constituting the import of the Vedas. A major definition of the meaning of ultimate things for him was rooted in the experience of Truth as outlined in the Vedas. We are therefore drawn into considering the scheme of values and norms and its effect in the cultural patterns that the Arya Samaj introduced into Hindu society in South Africa. Clyde Kluckohn's use of the term "culture" expresses this quite clearly. He sees culture as all those historically created designs for living, explicit and implicit, rational, irrational and non-rational, that exist at any given time as potential guides for the behaviour of men.

By breaking away from the traditional patterns of conduct, Dayananda demonstrated how clearly he sensed the need for reorientation of the concept of values and their interplay on culture. As goals, values are those states or objects towards which behaviour is preferentially directed. Religion as a primary source of values is affected by social content. For Arya Samaj, religion is the primary starting point. The criteria for change are valued in terms of the effect that religious training may have in the social context involving succeeding generations.

Bearing in mind that for Dayananda Vedic Truth underlay all religious and social behaviour, we view the scientific study of the values that Truth engendered as the framework for total religious commitment. The relationship between religious influence and social change serves as the summary of the ideals that conceptualise for people the more lasting influences for society in the context of such religious commitment.

CHAPTER 1

Aryan Benevolent Home

THE FOUNDER PRESIDENT of the Arya Yuvak Sabha Mr. D.G. Satyadeva is remembered by all persons interested in the Arya Samaj as one of the stalwarts of the movement in this country. Not only was he responsible for the birth of the Arya Yuvak Sabha, he was also one of the founders of the Arya Pratinidhi Sabha. It was, however, one very brief but poignant scene that fate played out in his life that was responsible for the coming into existence of one of South Africa's greatest achievements in the field of social welfare for any population group in the country. The Aryan Benevolent Home ranks as one of this community's proud achievements particularly in that area of social work dealing with care of the aged and orphans.

An African constable was seen one night in April 1918 violently abusing an old and frail Indian beggar who, "out of necessity had rested his weary limbs by the roadside."[1] The homeless beggar sought shelter in a nearby public toilet. This incident invoked the sympathy of the man who remembered the lessons of the Arya Samaj movement which appealed to men to understand that, "The prime object of the Arya Samaj—Vedic Church, is to do good to the world, that is, to promote physical, spiritual and social good of every sentient being."[2] "All men should subordinate themselves to the laws of society calculated to promote the well-being of all."[3]

The incident was related to members of the Arya Yuvak Sabha at its meeting on the 7th July 1918. A resolution calling for the establishment of the Aryan Benevolent Home was then adopted. The first home established in Mayville to accommodate people in need of care was known as Arya Anath Ashram. Then followed the purchase of the property at Bellair Road in Mayville in December 1918. Public donations were called for and through wise leadership the place of refuge and safety grew in size and strength. By 1924 the Ashram was well-known not only to the general public but also to government and civic bodies. The Protector of Indian Immigrants was known to send Indians in need of assistance to the home. Later, even the police were able to send people such as loiterers and potential criminals there. In 1926, there were 26 inmates and the Home realised the need for opening its doors to orphans and other children in need of care.[4] The building grew in size over the years. The original wood and iron building was replaced by a solid brick building that was extended in 1928, again in 1935 and 1943.[5]

On 1 May 1965, the aged were transferred to the Clayton Gardens Home at Asherville after negotiations with the City Council. The activities of the Home had to be more clearly defined as both aged and young children were being cared for. On June 22, 1965 the Aryan Benevolent Home Council decided to form two separate units, namely a Children's Home and a Home for the Aged, each with a separate Board of Management.[6]

The Children's Home now situated in Chatsworth, the sprawling Indian township south of Durban, was completed in June 1979 and the children moved into their new cottage a month later. The senior citizens were able to move to their new home, named the Dayananda Gardens Home for the Aged in 1982, the "Year of the Aged". The commemorative brochure published on the occasion mentions the three men primarily responsible for its early growth and development. These were Mr. D.G. Satyadeva, Mr. Nayanah Rajh and Mr. S.L. Singh.[7] The three men worked in earnest to induce a more charitable attitude of service of the less fortunate. Many others were inspired by the dedication of the three men and contributed to the growth of the movement. Like the founders, they showed a high sense of responsibility and became a link in the successful operation of the home in the various stages of its growth in the last sixty years.[8]

At the time of the transfer from the old Clayton Gardens Home to the new Dayananda Gardens Home for the Aged in Chatsworth, some one hundred and sixty residents were moved to the impressive new building. Some four thousand frail, sick and lonely aged residents have received comfort at the Home, which serves those in most need of care. Some residents still live at the old premises at Clayton Gardens, but the building in Cato Manor no longer exists.[9]

The organisation that brought the Aryan Benevolent Home into existence was Arya Yuvak Sabha. A diagramatic representation of the Sabha and its subsidiaries is presented below:[10]

ARYA YUVAK SABHA

ARYAN BENEVOLENT HOME COUNCIL

BOARDS OF MANAGEMENT

CLAYTON HOME FOR THE AGED	DAYANANDA HOME FOR THE AGED	DAYANANDA HOME FOR CHILDREN
RESIDENTS COMMITTEE	ADMISSION AND WELFARE COMMITTEE	CLINICAL SUB-COMMITTEE
	DAY SERVICE CENTRE	

STANDING COMMITTEES

FINANCE AND DEVELOPMENT	STAFFING AND SALARIES

The three homes are served by two Boards of Management: A Children's Home Board of Management and the Home for the Aged Board of Management. The transfer of residents to Dayananda Gardens in Chatsworth just before the home was opened by the Mayor of Durban on the 6 November 1982 was carried out by members of the Civil Defence, with the aid of buses supplied by the Durban City Council. The programme for the day consisted of speeches, songs, goodwill messages from government officials, unveiling of plaques and foundation stones for the various wards. The transfer of one hundred and sixty residents, some on stretchers and others in wheel chairs was done with great efficiency. The stay of residents at the new home does, however, offer many challenges in the care of the aged and also care of orphans.

Social Work Services

Side by side with nursing and medical care, the services of trained social workers, occupational therapists and physiopsychiatric personnel are available to meet the needs of 236 geriatrics and other aged persons. This poses a great challenge to the home because of the limited resources available at provincial, State and University hospitals. Any voluntary assistance by private practitioners is greatly appreciated.[11]

The Home has the services at present of three trained and qualified social workers. Social work services include:

i. Admission
ii. Counselling
iii. Administration of Grants
iv. Problem solving
v. Contact with relatives
vi. Liaison

Casework	*Group work*	*Community Work*
Intake and	Activities	Education
screening	Self-awareness	Hobbies
referral services	groups	Meals
Liaison		Music
		Group discussions
		Remunerative
		Employment
		Outings

Nursing and Medical Care

The residents of the Home for the Aged are divided into three categories:

A Category	residents are social pensioners
B Category	patients are referred to as "Frail Aged"
C Category	patients as "Very Frail Aged"

The Home contains one hundred and sixteen hospital beds allocated to five wards, four of which contain twenty-four beds each, while the fifth has twenty beds and serves as an intensive care unit. Each ward is divided into three bays with eight beds each, and is managed by trained sisters and staff nurses. Modern facilities such as communication safety measures are provided in the bathrooms and toilets. A medical dispensary is an additional feature and the modern design of the wards and bays makes nursing care easier, with the emphasis on individual attention to patients.[12]

The Home is visited regularly by a doctor. Several doctors have offered voluntary service so services are given on a time-shared basis. Patients are also sent to local hospitals such as the R.K. Khan,

Wentworth, King Edward and King George V. The Aryan Benevolent Home, like other similar institutions, is studying the problem of ageing and makes a critical evaluation of the problems encountered. Studies in gerontology and geriatric medical care have contributed considerably to solutions to the problems, and have also assisted in the care and attention given to geriatrics in the Home. Representatives from the Home contribute considerably to discussions at seminars and conferences which are held in all parts of the country. Some of the problems being encountered in this field of study are accumulated pathological difficulties, cataracts, arthritis, cerebral vascular accidents, congestive cardiac failure, diabetes and hemoplegia. Physiotherapy and related treatment are given and these services are being expanded.[13]

CHILDREN'S HOME

The Children's Home was established at 186 Bellair Road—Mayville in 1921. This contributed to the versatility of the Aryan Benevolent Home as it became the only organisation to provide institutional care for children as well as adults, and extended its services to assist other welfare agencies. The year 1979 was regarded as unique for two reasons. Not only was it declared the "Year of the Child" it was also the year the institution took possession of its brand new building in which the children are now housed.

The children are admitted only on the recommendation of the Department of Internal Affairs which is the chief supporting agent for finance. The children are drawn from primarily Hindu and Christian backgrounds and all their needs are met as they would be in any normal home and family situation. The children are expected to stay until they reach the age of eighteen or completion of high school. In some cases marriages have been arranged and performed according to their religious backgrounds. Strict religious life is encouraged with Arya Samaj doctrines being emphasized. No attempt is ever made to convert the children to the Hindu faith nor are they enticed to become Arya Samajists.

REFERENCES

1. Souvenir Brochure, Aryan Benevolent Home, 1982.
2. The Sixth Principle of Arya Samaj.

3. The Tenth Principle of Arya Samaj.
4. Souvenir Brochure, Aryan Benevolent Home, 1982.
5. *Ibid.*
6. Souvenir Brochure, 1982.
7. Souvenir Brochure, 1982.
8. Souvenir Brochure, 1982.
9. Souvenir Brochure, 1982.
10. Souvenir Brochure, 1982.
11. This information was received through interviews with the Social Workers and other persons.
12. Fifty-third Annual Report, Published 26 July 1975.
13. Secretarial Report, 29 June 1980.

CHAPTER 2

Subsidiary Institutions

WHEN IN 1950 the Arya Pratinidhi Sabha celebrated its twenty-fifth year of existence, no less than fourteen branch units had been declared member units in Durban and a further ten were affiliated in various parts of Natal. At the time of the formation of the Arya Pratinidhi Sabha in 1925 at least one of these the Ved Dharma Sabha of Pietermaritzburg had been in existence for more than a decade. Pietermaritzburg had been a centre of vibrant religious consciousness and many very devout and ardent Arya Samajists, directly influenced by the flood of Aryan activities in the Punjab in India, started the work in Natal's capital city. The Ved Dharma Sabha was started in 1909. In addition to these twenty-four Arya Samaj affiliates, the Arya Yuvak Sabha of Durban and the Aryan Benevolent Home, large and formidable institutions in their own rights, were accepted, bringing the total number of affiliated units to twenty-six.

ARYAN YOUTH LEAGUE

The Aryan Youth League serves as a vehicle for cultural expression among Hindu youth. The tendency among people to view with pride the aspirations of youth for their cultural and religious well-being is fairly widespread. The history of the Arya Samaj movement having progressed along a course of development in which it attended to every aspect of social, cultural and religious life, it was inevitable that specific intentions for the young people in the community would surface before long.

VEDA NIKETAN

The Veda Niketan is the branch of the organisation which publishes its books and other suitable literature and also conducts examinations for students showing an interest in Hinduism.

VEDIC PUROHIT MANDAL

The Vedic Purhohit Mandal is the Academy of Vedic Priests founded by the Arya Samaj. The Mandal has formulated a code of religious procedure which all priests of the Sabha are expected to follow. It trains young men and women for their tasks as priests ministering to the community at large.

SECTION SIX

SOCIO-RELIGIOUS RECONSTRUCTION

Introduction

We now consider some of the salient features of socio-religious interaction in the Arya Samaj context. We do so while attempting to deal with the problem of socialization and more particularly the problems that confront the movement during the process of social action. We bear in mind firstly that social action in the context in which we discuss it here has necessarily to operate at the cultural level. In this context the superordinate meaning system accounts for the values and norms of interaction in the socialization process.

Religious socialization in our study is a focal point of consideration because of the reciprocal role relationship that exists in the interaction process. Swami Dayananda's insight into the modality of being as the broad framework for social restructuring has not enabled the process to be undertaken with effectiveness but its lasting applications outside the framework of the specific context for which such modality had been conceived has become an effective basis for socialization per se.

Our concern with the fundamental effectiveness of religion as the prime mover in social interaction impinges upon the techniques of causal interaction. As such it may be pertinent to ask if a force as cause once set in motion may become part of a complex of causes that mutually condition each other. If so, it becomes an important part of the explanation of social change albeit intended for one setting but subsequently consequential in another.

Our task is to discover the conditions which influence change and which pin point the general points of influence which both maximise and minimize such socialization. The emerging pattern as we shall see in this section is the ability of religion to effect the process of social change. A degree of autonomy is inevitable if any religious institution is to prove effective. We state then in the context of this study that religious socialization becomes an integral part of the movement because the process of socialization is primarily religious socialization and not a social process independent of the religious process in which such socialization takes place.

The ascendancy of spiritual motives is the underlying key to progressive control of the values in which the objectives of religious action are seen to operate. The Arya Samaj movement in South Africa is entirely motivated within the local context in which the movement operates. The process of socialization is effected in two contexts. Firstly in the writings of the founder of the movement, whose general framework of social change is a prescription for action in the context in which we see the developments taking place and secondly in the conditions of change existing in the social context under discussion. Talcott Parsons[1] discusses at least one aspect of the process of socialization occurring within a specific context.

Yinger[2] believes that the functional interdependence of religion in society is strongly motivated resulting in a degree of religious change becoming inevitable in the process. Our purpose enables us to linger on the functional modality of change resulting from religious motivation as an initiator of change. The Arya Samaj movement, and more particularly the leaders within the movement in this country, would readily admit that while the teachings motivated within the movement focus on the need for modifications of approach to religious action, beliefs and general group structure are inevitably affected by social changes in a reciprocal process.

There is one fundamental element of the structural modality that the Arya Samaj has intended to maintain in the hope of a lasting influence upon a society that was in need of change. The fundamental elements of the Arya Samaj faith appeared at first to circumscribe the areas of religious action in which radical influence was necessary. The important elements of religion for the Arya Samaj have been clearly indicated and all social interaction had necessarily to occur within the framework of such limitation. The roots of Arya Samaj theology as we have stressed throughout, are inextricably merged in Vedic doctrine. As such, they would ordinarily not brook any form of excessive modification. But our study has already outlined what need there has been for a mutual interaction between Arya Samaj theology and Hindu doctrine in general, resulting in an acceptable modification enhancing Hindu perspective in a wider sphere of influence.

We entertain the theory that religion, as we have thus far understood the term, is an essential part of the machinery of law, morality and functional interchange. As such it provides the framework, however complex this may be in some situations, for human interaction to take place at a religious level, while at the same time providing a basis for socio-cultural action enabling members of a particular segment of society to live together in an orderly arrangement of social relations as outlined by a specific doctrine.

This then is for us the basis for discussion. How the doctrines that influence behaviour patterns become the basis for the social function of religion, and how these doctrines provide for the maintenance of social order are the problems we consider.[3]

REFERENCES

1. Parsons, T., *The Social System*, The Free Press, Illinois, 1949.
2. Yinger, M., *Religion, Society and the Individual*, MacMillan, New York, 1957, p. 266.
3. Radcliffe-Brown, A.R., *Religion and Society, Religion and Culture and Society*, ed. Louis Schneider, Wiley and Sons, New York, 1964.

CHAPTER 1

Impact on Religion, Education and Culture

THE COMING OF the Arya Samaj movement to South Africa has been of considerable religious, educational and cultural significance to the Hindu community. This is indicated by several features of religious thought encountered in the plan of action that was envisaged by the founders of the movement. The draft constitution of the Arya Pratinidhi Sabha contains an important aim in the form of a clause which reads:[1]

> "To establish, build and maintain schools, halls, temples, libraries, ashrams, gymnasia, warehouses, offices and flats in the interest of the Sabha."

The founders of the movement, having been made aware of the call for a total restructuring of educational ideas by Swami Dayananda and having been inspired by the achievement of the Samaj in India with the establishment of its Gurukuls and the Dayananda Anglo-Vedic College, decided to embark on a programme of service that would include the establishment of schools in various parts of Natal.

The decision to establish educational institutions in India resulted in considerable impact being made in later years by Arya Samaj schools upon the whole educational system in that country. Rudolph and Rudolph,[2] for example, describe this by saying that: "The education activities of the Arya Samaj, a militant Hindu reform organisation, illustrate how social reform movements within Hinduism used education to express their cultural norms and identity. The Arya Samaj sought to strengthen Hinduism against its Christian and Muslim competitors by emphasizing the unity of Hinduism found in early Vedic materials."

We have already explained why two types of educational institutions were brought into existence to carry out this work in education. One was the Gurukula, patterned on the ancient educational institutions of the same name which laid stress on the study of Hindu literature, and the other the conventional college which Arya Samaj named the Dayanand Anglo-Vedic College.

At the time of the establishment of the Arya Pratinidhi Sabha in South Africa, educational opportunities for the Indian community were extremely limited due to the shortage of schools, teachers and equipment. An Education Commission appointed in 1909 drew attention to the grave depravations suffered by Indians in Natal,[3] namely overcrowding and a shortage of schools and trained teachers. The position in 1925 was not much different. The history of Indian education in this country is a record of the unquestionably difficult situation which prevailed from 1869, when the first school for Indians offering education in English was placed under the control of the Natal Education Department.[4]

The story of Indian education, tragic as it had been for the greater part of the history of the Indian people in this country, is heightened by the intense conflict within the community concerning the choice between religiously oriented education and secular education. Most of the Indian people, particularly Hindus and Muslims,were bound to traditional forms of dress and other cultural patterns of life. Although provision was made for the preservation of Indian modes of life in the secular education provided by the Indian Immigrant School Board,[5] fears began to grow and soon there were expressions of strong feelings about "westernisation" of the Indian community being effected through English medium education.[6]

Oosthuizen and Hofmeyr make the point that the state made no provision for children who in habit and dress did not adhere to Western standards, and that education was used as an instrument to destroy the customs of the Indian child.[7]

This engendered a situation of conflict, for quite clearly the Indians' desire for education enforced the provision of schools by the community itself in the form of state-aided schools in which secular education was provided while the desire for the preservation of religious ideals necessitated the provision of religious education. Behr and Macmillan tell us that in 1882 there were no state schools for the Indian community (the first was built in 1883) whereas ten state-aided schools were functioning with an enrolment of 323 students. In 1893 there were 2 state schools (with a total of 340 students) as compared with 24 state-aided schools with an enrolment of 2249 pupils. State schools are schools built by the state; state-aided schools were built by the Indian community sometimes with state assistance.

The Arya Pratinidhi Sabha's decision to establish schools where Hindi and all aspects of Hindu culture could be imparted proved extraordinarily difficult. The establishment of schools involved the provision of school buildings, equipment and teachers, the costs of which proved in many instances to be beyond the means of the community. Nevertheless, many attempts were made with varying degrees of success. In all instances where "success" was achieved the type of education provided was never subject to examination by a board of educationists as was the case with government schools under the control of a Board of Education.

The education provided by the Hindu community took the form of stories, discourses and incidents from the *Rāmāyaṇa* and *Mahābhārata*. None of the teachers had had any formal training so this soon proved a formidable problem.[8] Two people who were largely responsible for initiating interest in Hindu education were Swami Shankarananda and Swami Bhawani Dayal. In 1917, the Second Hindu Literary Conference was held in Pietermaritzburg. Subsequently "a few schools to impart Hindi" were brought into existence.[9]

A Hindi school consisting of 220 pupils, divided into six standards was conducted under the direction of the Sabha.[10] It has been established that many of the Vedic institutions affiliated to the Arya Pratinidhi Sabha attempted to establish Hindi schools. It is however, difficult to state exactly what was meant by a Hindi school because these could vary from a class of one or two pupils under the direction of a teacher meeting in the lounge of a private house to a class of many children meeting in a classroom in a state-aided school building.

The Arya Yuvak Mandal of Sea Cow Lake started its school for vernacular education in 1912.[11]

On 20 September 1921 the Arya Samaj in Cato Manor established a school and in 1931 another building was erected by the same organisation.[12]

The Arya Samaj of Ladysmith opened its school in 1921 through the assistance of local supporters of the movement.[13]

In January 1931 the Candella Estate Hindi Sangathan was formed. The organisation erected a large school building, the foundation stone of which was laid by the then Mayoress of Durban.[14] The school, for girls only, was erected for the purpose of providing Hindi education.

The Yuvak Arya Samaj of Clairwood in 1933 erected a school

building for the provision of Hindi education.[15]

The Arya Mitra Mandal of Sydenham opened a Hindi school in 1940. This Mandal is of the organisations that allowed its school to be "held at the homes of the members" of the organisation. In 1942 the Essendene Road Indian School was used to impart Hindi education.[16]

The Arya Samaj of Mount Partridge constructed its school building in 1943 on land donated by a local public spirited member of the Arya Samaj.[17]

The Vedic Yuvak Sabha of Wilgefontein conducted a school at the homes of its members. A school building was erected in 1943 from donations made by its members.[18]

The Arya Yuvak Sabha of Raisethorpe in Pietermaritzburg was able to build a school with financial assistance from the Natal Provincial Administration. The school was opened in 1945 and as it grew in size well-wishers in the community contributed funds for the extension of the building.[19] The Vedic Vidya Pracharak Sabha of Pentrich in Pietermaritzburg built a school in 1932 which provided education for 250 children. The building was considerably extended a year later when additional classrooms were added.[20]

On 28 July 1946 the Arya Samaj at Westville opened the doors of its school building to children of the Hindu community.[21]

The Nagari Pracharni Sabha of Springfield has had its school building used for both Hindi and English education as a Government-aided school since 1940.

The emphasis placed on Hindi education by the community enabled many dedicated persons to assist in the provision of educational facilities whereby Hindi was taught to the children. The work of the Arya Samaj movement was thus of considerable importance, as evidenced by the number of Arya Samaj organisations that collected funds and provided facilities for both Hindi and English education. However, the community laboured under several difficulties. In addition to lack of trained teachers, the number of people inspired by the ideas of the Arya Samaj and by the Gurukulas and D.A.V. Colleges in India, was very small. The influence of the Arya Samaj, however, was felt in the inspiration it provided for the establishment of schools for the express purpose of providing religious education. With the failure on the part of the government to provide secular, English-medium education, these schools had to be converted from vernacular schools to English schools, thus bringing about a change in emphasis in the kind of education provided for the community.[22]

A process of secularization was initiated in the Hindu community by the education system it was forced to inherit largely through the Cape Town Agreement of 1927. This stressed that Indians would be made to feel more welcome in South Africa if they accepted western standards of life. This was one of the factors that initiated a process of change of outlook on cultural matters within the community. At present considerable changes in the economic position of Indians sees these changes escalating even more.[23] Many members of the community now face the daunting task of combining modern education in which secular values are emphasized, with religious interests which receive little doctrinal guidance or support.

The impact of the Arya Samaj is nevertheless being felt due to its regular religious services. Several people who were interviewed contributed views on the growth of the Arya Samaj and its influence upon the community. We record some of the salient points arising from these interviews.

Mr. S.R. was of the view that the Arya Samaj movement filled the gap created by the severe restrictions placed upon Hindu brides entering South Africa.[24] The difficulty placed on preachers in a similar way, added considerably, he believed, to the work of the Arya Samaj movement. He commented that at least half the eminent visitors to this country from India in the last fifty years were Arya Samajists. The contribution of the Arya Samaj to the cultural endeavours of the Hindu community as a whole, he saw, therefore, as unique.

Mr. P.H. was interviewed because he is a graduate of the Gurukul Kangri. This is one of the best known schools of the Arya Samaj in India. Mr. P.H. was a student there between 1927 and 1941, which means that he spent his entire school life at Arya Samaj educational institutions. The primary and secondary school phases were completed at Gurukul Indraprastha and tertiary education at Gurukul Kangri. The Gurukul Kangri, a tertiary level college, was for a time an affiliate of the Punjab University. Among the subjects he studied was the ancient system of medicine, Ayurveda, recognised by the government of India as a legitimate scientific medical system. P.H. studied through the medium of Hindi although Sanskrit and English were compulsory subjects. In addition, he completed studies in History, Geography, Chemistry, Physics and Hinduism. One was able to learn from this interview that no degrees as such were conferred upon graduates but the ancient tutelary titles like Vedālaṅkār, for graduates in Arts, Science, Politics and Religion; Āyurvedālaṅkār for graduates in Āyurveda; Siddhāntālaṅkār for graduates in Hindu Theology and Philosophy; Vidyālaṅkār for graduates in Economics and Vidyāvācas for graduates in Law, were conferred.

Mr. P.H. was proud of the fact that he had studied at the institutions named, because of their unique character. He was convinced that no school or college in South Africa would have enabled him to develop the wide breadth of outlook he had on all aspects of life. He was initially inspired, he says, by Professor Bhai Parmanand. Despite the fact that very few students have gone to India for studies at the Arya Samaj schools, he was of the view that their influence upon religious thinking in South Africa was very significant. Thus, many of the Hindu organisations that came into existence subsequently were not necessarily Arya Samaj in name, but were certainly Arya Samaj inspired.

Mr. R.B. of Johannesburg studied at the Gurukul Sūpa from 1939 to 1946. For him, the Gurukul system attained very high standards of education and inspired students to be very highly motivated. He was extremely happy to have been part of a unique educational system which required of students a very high standard of moral, ethical and religious behaviour. For this reason, the young students were called Brahmacāris. They were required to shave their heads leaving only a tuft of hair on the crown which symbolised limited attachment to the world. They were largely required to sever all worldly connections until a full educational programme had been completed.

The school routine commenced at 5 a.m. everyday with a bath in cold water and washing of clothes. Morning prayers required chanting Vedic mantras, Sandhyā-havan, followed by Yoga Āsanas, and then breakfast. The students followed a very strict vegetarian diet.

Sandhyā and prayers involving havan were conducted everyday. Classes closed at 4.00 p.m. and a strenuous sports programme was conducted for boys who were keen, particularly in cricket, hockey and swimming. The subjects studied included History, Geography, Science and Mathematics—all through the medium of Hindi. In addition, there were studies in Gujarati, English and Sanskrit. Every student was instilled with a pride in, and love for, Hindu culture

Nationalistic feelings were also inculcated and every student was known as a proud nationalist. This was a boys' school that attempted to remain true to the ancient tradition of Hindu cultural life. Even the food that was consumed was always Sātvic in content. He was proud to have been part of an international community during his stay at the school for in addition to the local boys there were many from other countries.

On Mr. R.B.'s return to South Africa he was admired by thousands of Hindus in this country for his ability to read, write and speak several Indian languages, including Sanskrit. It is, however, his contribution to the cultural life of the community that is considered admirable. He became the first president of a Hindu economic movement in the Transvaal, was President of a provincial Gujarati organisation and an official of a national one. His studies enabled him to acquire a very broad and national outlook. He maintains a deep interest in cultural and religious matters despite involvement in his own thriving business. His insight into the Hindu scriptures makes him one of the foremost students of Hinduism in South Africa.

Pandit H.A. of Johannesburg is also a graduate of Gurukul Supa. He is proud of the fact that Arya Samaj work is now being done by the Government of India which has adopted as national policy many of the reforms introduced by the Arya Samaj movement.

He lives in Johannesburg and is a very influential religious leader who spreads Arya Samaj principles among people in the Transvaal. He advocates all that Arya Samaj stands for, such as declaring Hindi the national language of India, allowing widows to remarry, and general social reconstruction through industry and commerce. He believes that the Government of India has introduced all these programmes of reform because they had already been adopted by the Arya Samaj.

Mr. H.A. believes that the establishment of the Arya Samaj in 1875 and its adoption of reforms enabled India to proceed along a very positive course of nation building which actually prepared the ground for the coming of Mahatma Gandhi, who easily adopted and later continued the programme of reconstruction which followed independence.

Mr. H.M. of Johannesburg, now 79 years old, was greatly influenced by the Arya Samaj. He was impressed by the lack of rigidity and the exclusion from society of caste prejudices. Although he was not a committed Arya Samajist he was deeply aware of its enormous influence upon the community. He thus gave open support to its programme of reform, particularly the call for equal education for girls. He openly supported the Gurukula system and encouraged many girls to join it. His influence enabled many girls from South Africa, particularly from the Transvaal, to go to India to join various Gurukulas.

He firmly believes that all Arya Samaj principles are very constructive and while aware of the prejudices that worked against the movement was one of its great supporters. He is a man of considerable influence in the Gujarati community in South Africa and is respected as a leader of his people.

Thus Arya Samaj, he felt, was responsible for bringing about modern education which encouraged breaking away from rigid orthodoxy and enhanced modernisation. He advocates equality for all, condemns caste and communal prejudices and holds Swami Dayananda in great esteem as a reformer whose influence has helped to make Hindu life in South Africa praiseworthy.

He is of the view that the initial opposition to the Arya Samaj was uncalled for. But initial opposition, to all reform movements he said was to be expected. People have a tendency to view with suspicion reforms of any kind. The initial response had necessarily to be hostile because of the Arya Samaj's open hostility to age-old practices within Hinduism. Idol worship, or what is regarded as such, is sometimes frowned on, but most people fail to appreciate the true value of worship in this form. Idol worship is the worship of God through the use of visual objects. The task of Arya Samaj is to learn to respect all forms of worship, because not only is this the common-sense thing to do, it is also part of Hindu life and thinking which advocates respect for all religions and also respect for all forms of worship.

Mrs. B. was less responsive in the interview but was happy to express her feelings concerning the broad outlook she developed as a student at the Gurukula Sūpa. She spent only about six years there, but learned much and was appreciative of the part played by that education in moulding her life. Her marriage has precluded her from taking an active part in community affairs but she has always given her whole-hearted support to every form of cultural, religious and educational innovation that has contributed to the good of the community.

Mr. B.G. of Port Elizabeth is a Gujarati-speaking gentleman dedicated to the Arya Samaj cause through the influence of his parents. He and an elder brother were sent to India by their parents in 1922 and enrolled at the Gurukula Sūpa near Navasari. He had been a student at the Gurukula for only six months when his elder brother contracted an incurable disease and died suddenly, whereupon his parents made him return home immediately. His commitment to Arya Samaj ideals has not diminished, however, and he has helped in every way possible to establish Arya Samaj work in the Eastern Cape. He contributed in a small way to the construction of the Hindu Temple in Port Elizabeth by the community. This was a mark of his dedication and a sample of the work being done in the province for Arya Samaj teachings.

The attempt to ascertain the number of people who belong to the Arya Samaj movement or who have in some way been influenced by its teachings was not very successful. The Secretary of the Arya Pratinidhi Sabha allowed the writer access to his records, but as the information in them was not based on any survey, the figures were not considered reliable. They were derived from reports submitted by affiliated organisations for the purpose of compiling an official report of the Arya Pratinidhi Sabha. Nearly one hundred thousand people from the four language groups within the Arya Samaj movement are members of the organisation or have been influenced by it in one way or another. This accounts for almost one-third of the Hindi-speaking people, approximately 10 per cent of the Gujarati-speaking people, two per cent of the Telugus and less than one per cent of the Tamils. The Arya Samaj message has been spread to a wide cross-section of the Hindi-speaking community and membership ranges from professionals to labourers from every economic and social background and from every class of society. The movement continues to spread because of the work being done by the organisation through its publications and more especially through visitors who came to this country as guest lecturers.

REFERENCES

1. Clause 3(b), "Draft of Revised Constitution of the Arya Pratinidhi Sabha of South Africa".

2. Rudolph, S.H. and Rudolph L.I., *Education and Politics in India from Studies in Organisation, Society and Policy*, Harvard University Press, Cambridge, 1972.

3. Behr, A.L. and MacMillan, R.G., *Education in South Africa*, Van Schaik, Pretoria, 1966, p. 336.

4. Behr, A.L., and MacMillan, *Ibid*, p. 336.

5. Coopan, S., *The Indian Community of South Africa: Past, Present and Future*, S.A. Institute of Race Relations, Johannesburg, 1960.
6. Oosthuizen, G.C. and Hofmeyr, J.H., *A Socio-Religious Survey of Chatsworth*, University of Durban-Westville, Durban, 1981, p. 21.
7. Agrawal, P.N., *Bhawani Dayal Sannyasi*, Indian Colonial Association Etawah N P, 1939.
8. Vedalankar, N., *Religious Awakening in South Africa*, p. 52.
9. *Ibid.*, p. 84.
10. *Ibid.*, p. 85.
11. *Ibid.*, p. 85.
12. *Ibid.*, p. 86.
13. *Ibid.*, p. 86.
14. *Ibid.*, p. 88.
15. *Ibid.*, p. 90.
16. *Ibid.*, p. 90.
17. *Ibid.*, p. 91.
18. *Ibid.*, p. 90.
19. *Ibid.*, p. 92.
20. *Ibid.*, p. 93.
21. *Ibid.*, p. 93.
22. *Ibid.*, p. 92.
23. *Ibid.*, p. 87.
24. Kuppusami, C, et Pillay, M.G., *Pioneer Footprints*, Nasau, Durban, 1978.

CHAPTER 2

Śuddhī and Society

THE ŚUDDHĪ CEREMONY initiated by the Arya Samaj played a significant role in reclaiming 100,000 Malkana Rajputs who had been converted to other faiths during the Moplah rebellion in Malabar in 1921. Since then, many hundreds of people have returned to the Hindu fold primarily due to the work of the Arya Samaj, even after the death of Dayananda.[1]

The Śuddhī Saṁskāra was introduced into South Africa almost immediately after the establishment of the Arya Yuvak Sabha. The bane of Hindu life both in India and elsewhere is the problem of conversion of Hindus to other faiths. Many millions have left the faith for reasons already described. Arya Samajists, like many other followers of Hindu movements, have been very perturbed by the work of Christian and Muslim missionaries. Poverty and ignorance within Hindu society have featured most prominently as reasons for this massive apostasy and considerable efforts have been made by Hindu organisations to counteract them.

Of the Hindu organisations in South Africa,[2] the Arya Pratinidhi Sabha has been most concerned with the problem. Its institution of the ceremony of Śuddhī Saṁskāra is the most important result of this concern.

Swami Shankarananda and Swami Bhawani Dayal were the first persons to carry out a campaign of reconversion in South Africa.[3] Swami Shankarananda instituted this ceremony in this country and then carried out a vigorous campaign to dissuade Hindus from converting to other faiths. The Śuddhī Saṁskāra is a religious rite, a purification ceremony, performed for all who return to the Hindu fold from religions to which they had been converted. This area of concern has featured prominently in discussions at Hindu conferences, e.g. the South African Hindu Maha Sabha conference held in May 1982.[4] A plea was made for the Śuddhī Saṁskāra to be retained and encouraged in the light of missionary activities in more recent years.

Dr. Hofmeyr's findings in a recent research project consider at some length the problem of conversion from Hinduism.[5] Hindus, he says, identify themselves as Hindus in terms of home language. The irony of this is that the home language of most Hindus in South Africa is English, with the result that most of this identification cannot be measured in specifically religious terms. The problem is exacerbated by a lack of sub-group (in this case language) identity. However, the work of neo-Hindu movements[6] does institute a new sense of identity among many Hindus with the result that belief in specific religious doctrines helps to replace the earlier forms of identification.

Prof. G.C. Oosthuizen, in his study of the work of the Pentecostal churches, raises the question of the reason for this form of Protestantism being so effective among the Hindu community, particularly in Metropolitan Durban.[7] His research has revealed several findings which Dr. Hofmeyr's work confirms. No doubt traditional forms of ritual Hinduism leave many Hindus with a sense of emptiness and lack of religious inspiration. Reasons that generally emerge show interesting facts concerning conversion to Christianity by Hindus. Many gave as their reasons, desire for greater economic wealth, while some converted for reasons of health. "Healing services" are a common method of enticement to Christianity. Other factors were marriage, conversion of relatives and some claimed to have "found the truth".

Hofmeyr's most significant finding is that Tamil and Telugu groups suffered the biggest losses to Christianity. Only 1.1 per cent of Hindi people had converted, as compared to 5.9 per cent of Tamils and 4.2 per cent of Telugus. There were no converts among Gujaratis. Converts came mainly from lower income groups and from those groups whose vernacular is least well preserved.[8]

Hofmeyr's comparison of the figures reflecting differences between the Durban suburbs of Chatsworth and Reservoir Hills is even more interesting. In Chatsworth, where the residents are of a lower economic standing, one in every five members of the Hindi community have been converted to Christianity, whereas Hindus in Reservoir Hills, who have a high economic standing, have produced one convert for every twenty residents. Hofmeyr says that "Pentecostalism does not flourish in the more affluent communities which also explains the fact that its impact has been less effective in the area under discussion." (The area under discussion being Reservoir Hills.)[9]

The Arya Samaj movement, together with other neo-Hindu

movements and others in South Africa, needs to take account of a significant comment by Dr. Hofmeyr. He says, "The future success of Hinduism in South Africa would appear to depend upon the extent to which neo-Hindu movements succeed in effecting real commitment from the Hindus in the environment in which most needs are satisfied by Western secular culture."[10]

The problem of conversion for most Hindu organisations rests with the problems of commitment and the resulting enthusiasm for work which emerges from such commitment. While it is true that Hinduism is not a proselytizing religion, it is also true that Hindus need to take cognisance of the facts of religious organisation and particularly administration.

The Śuddhī Saṁskāra is a purificatory rite. The act of purification, however, Arya Samajists would say, is an act by which men confirm that they would lead "pure" lives. By purity is understood living a clean wholesome life with no indulgence in illicit or extramarital sex, no drinking of alcoholic liquors, no smoking, trying to observe strict vegetarianism and observing all the other moral and ethical codes that go with belief in the eternal truths of the Vedas. The Śuddhī ceremony is therefore not meant primarily for people who reconvert to Hinduism but for all people who have "strayed" as it were from the path of Dharma as advocated by the Vedas.

Thus the Śuddhī ceremony is performed for all people who wish to participate in such a rite if they have had problems about maintaining faith in the religion into which they were born. The Śuddhī ceremony, however, has come to be associated with converts because of the emphasis placed upon the ceremony in their case. It was, however, never intended that the ceremony was an act of cleansing in the sense that people who had embraced other faiths were regarded as unclean. The Śuddhī Saṁskāra was a formal rite by which converts were reminded of their religious disabilities as advocated by Hinduism and in this way more meaningful religious commitment was solicited.

REFERENCES

1. Sharma, D.S., *Hinduism Through the Ages*, Bhawans, Bombay, 1956.

2. The South African Hindu Maha Sabha, The Arya Pratinidhi Sabha of South Africa, The Saiva Siddhanta Sangum of South Africa, The Ramakrishna Centre of South Africa, The Divine Life Society of South Africa.

3. Vedalankar, N., *Religious Awakening in South Africa*, p. 48.

4. Naidoo, T., *Challenge*, S.A. Hindu Maha Sabha, Durban, 1982.
5. Hofmeyr, J.H., *Religion in a South African Indian Community*, University of Durban-Westville, Durban, 1981.
6. See note 2.
7. Oosthuizen, G.C., *Pentecostal Penetration into the Indian Community in Metropolitan Durban*, HSRC, Pretoria, 1975.
8. Hofmeyr and Oosthuizen, *Ibid*, p. 5.
9. Hofmeyr and Oosthuizen, *Ibid*, p. 7.
10. Hofmeyr and Oosthuizen, *Ibid*, p. 8.

CHAPTER 3

Status of Women

THE ADVANCES made by the Arya Samaj movement in South Africa in religious reformation came as a result of the advances it achieved in other areas of life such as education. The religious conception among Hindi-speaking people throughout Natal was to alter radically from old obsolete ideas to reformed ones which introduced modified modes of worship and religious behaviour. It was considered by many that the impact of the ideas spread, not necessarily by the movement per se, but by the gospel it preached. Arya Samajists soon realised the value of spreading the message through the medium of English which was understood by most people. Soon women became a focal part of the Samaj's doctrinal hopes.

The first school for Indians offering education in English was opened, as Behr and Macmillan point out, in 1869.[1] Their report of a statement by the then Superintendent of Education is very significant. He stated that "Indians refused to have their girls taught to read."[2] The position concerning the education of women changed little for a long time. Forty years later there were 3284 Indians at both primary and secondary schools in Natal and of this number only 324 were girls.[3] Indian parents for a very long time considered the education of girls unnecessary. The following table gives an indication of the number of males and females at school in Natal between 1869 and 1886.

TABLE

YEAR	BOYS	GIRLS	SCHOOLS
1869	34	Nil	3
1871	69	10	3
1875	180	20	5
1881	206	22	7
1885	1400	223	12
1886	1428	274	25

Rambiritch concludes that Indian parents did not regard education for girls as much of an asset.[4] They would not allow their daughters to mix with boys or be taught by male teachers. Because Indian education was still in its infancy it was not feasible to establish separate schools for girls. Most of the girls attending school were Christian. Hindu and Muslim parents remained conservative in their attitudes.

These figures show only the attendances at primary schools. In 1930, only 7 girls were enrolled at secondary schools in Natal. In 1952 the number had increased to 666.[5]

The problem of education for girls occupied the minds of several educationists. An inspector of education in the Indian Immigrant School Board, which controlled Indian education before it passed to the jurisdiction of the Natal Education Department, suggested that schools under the direction of European women teachers might be a solution.[6] A further suggestion was that Indian women teachers be imported from India. In 1889, the first Indian woman teacher from India came to work at a school established by the St. Aidan's Mission.[7] There was a gradual change of attitude, and by 1895 there was less opposition to the education of Indian women but still not much enthusiasm for it either.[8]

At the time of the formation of the Arya Pratinidhi Sabha in 1925, few Indian women in South Africa had received any secondary or tertiary education. The gradual introduction of education among them came about only when serious rethinking on the matter occurred within the community over a protracted period of time. Eventually some women who wished to follow their talents to higher levels of advancement, were allowed an education at secondary and tertiary level. The tendency to allow women more freedom to pursue their interests in education was a slow process initially.

The University of Natal first admitted Indian women in 1936.[9] Their status began to change and soon they began to be recognised as free and independent persons with wishes and aspirations of their own. Hilda Kuper described their position: "Indian women are generally considered extensions of their husbands, but the more highly educated women are rated by their own accomplishments. Their status is a personal achievement sometimes attained in the face of strong family opposition and until a few years back in face of strong social opposition."[10] Within the Arya Samaj movement opposition was reduced to a minimum because of its advocacy of emancipation of women in all walks of life.

In 1947, forty-seven girls attended secondary schools throughout Natal. In 1955 the number had swelled to 781. By 1959 thirty women had obtained Bachelor of Arts Degrees at Natal University; one had a Master's degree, eleven were doctors and two were lawyers.[11] Since 1960 the number of female students at universities in South Africa has increased at the rate of 14.4 per cent, while male enrolment had grown by 9.9 per cent per annum. As a result, females represented a growing proportion of the total student population, increasing from 11 per cent in 1960 to 22.3 per cent in 1974.[12] The establishment of the University of Durban-Westville has been a major factor in the educational advancement of Indian women in South Africa. The number of females at the University of Durban-Westville increased from 30.1 per cent in 1974 at 35.4 per cent in 1980 and is likely to exceed 50 per cent in 1990.[13]

The Arya Samaj was one of the first Hindu religious organisations to openly advocate the education of women and girls. The increase in the number of professionally active women is partly due to the encouragement received from this quarter. The visit to the country by members of the Arya Kanya Mahavidyalaya in July 1934 helped considerably to enhance the changed status of women and girls who from then on began to exert stronger pressures for changes in attitudes.[14]

One outcome of the tremendous increase in the number of women graduates in the Hindu community is that traditional patterns of life, particularly in the domestic field, are expected to undergo enormous changes. Education, particularly the kind of western education that Indians receive in South Africa, has a definite effect on religion and religious attitudes. For example, whereas the mother in the family used to be responsible in most homes for the ritual practices associated with worship, the new educational backdrop that now features in many homes, with mother and daughters graduating from college and university, means that ritual religion will undoubtedly be subjected to drastic rethinking. While older people may adopt sympathetic attitudes to these practices younger people are less likely to do so. The change in the attitudes results from demands by young people for a new system of religious training, involving totally new religious ideas, values, norms and teachings.

At present, by far the most significant role specifically assigned to women within the movement is the priesthood. Arya Samaj women have been ordained as priestesses in considerable numbers, most of them having come from the many Arya Stri Samajs affiliated to the Arya Pratinidhi Sabha. Arya Stri Samaj, as the name indicates, is an Arya Samaj for women only and within this organisation considerable effort was directed at alleviating their problems.

Two women members of the Arya Pratinidhi Sabha were interviewed at some length for their views concerning the role of women in society. The first interviewee was a woman of considerable standing because of her notable contribution to the Arya Samaj cause. She is also an ordained priest with considerable experience in religious work, having officiated at a large number of weddings and other ceremonies. Her views on the emancipation of women have been a source of inspiration to many members of the Samaj.

Both women interviewed were extremely proud of the achievements of the Arya Samaj. The introduction of women to the priesthood and other leading religious activities was one of the main reasons for their own realisation of their neglect of religious responsibilities and how a new religious consciousness could be reintroduced into their own homes. Not only was Arya Samaj influence being felt throughout South Africa but both interviewees felt highly optimistic about its international growth, particularly in countries where Hindus had settled in large numbers. They felt that the coming of Swami Dayananda meant a rebirth of Hinduism as never before. This was particularly significant because Hindu missionaries were becoming increasingly aware of the serious neglect of Hindu religious and cultural ideals.

Arya Samaj influence in South Africa brought the obnoxious practices of child marriage and to a less extent the caste system to an end. While it was easy enough to influence Hindu thinking on marriageable ages, particularly for girls, the problem of caste, especially in the Gujarati community, was more difficult. Arya Samaj influence was, however, responsible for educating Hindus to the belief that even if the caste structure was to be retained the caste prejudices that often accompanied caste distinction were unnecessary. Among Hindi people the bride's practice of wearing a veil at her wedding was common. All Arya Samaj weddings were soon to rule out this practice and brides took to raising their heads while the sacred rite was being performed.

The Arya Samaj was the first organisation to openly advocate widow remarriage which meant that many Hindu women in South

Africa were no longer confined to a life of seclusion enforced by age-old traditions. The dowry system which was also introduced into South Africa was totally banned by the Arya Samaj. The system had obtained in India for centuries bringing untold hardships to many families. The system which required the bride's parents to place large sums of money, jewellery and other possessions in the care of the groom before a marriage could be solemnised, left many families in deep debt for many years after the marriage, thus making them virtual slaves to a system they neither loved nor supported but followed only to satisfy the whims of a customary practice that had no logical explanation.

Both women interviewed felt that some of these practices had their origins in the religious books that Swami Dayananda condemned and were happy with Arya Samaj influence in having them removed.

The interviewees spoke with pride on the role played by many women in the Hindu community whose emancipation led to their leading happy lives. Because of this women came to the fore in playing leading roles in community affairs, especially through joining the priesthood and numerous other professions such as education, medicine, law, etc.

Another interviewee who did not belong to the Arya Pratinidhi Sabha was a former student at an Arya Samaj Gurukula in India. She will be referred to here as Mrs. K.D. of Johannesburg. She was among the first Hindu women in South Africa to receive a secondary education. She was sent to India by her parents and enrolled at the famous Arya Kanya Mahavidyalya girls' school in Baroda. This was a Gujarati-medium school which was chosen because Mrs. K.D. was Gujarati-speaking. She went to India in 1935 in the company of several other girls and boys whose families were inspired by the Arya Samaj call to rejuvenate and re-educate young people to the new values it advocated. Mrs. K.D. spent seven years at the Gurukula before returning to South Africa to become one of a new breed of emancipated women.

Mrs. K.D. described her stay in India as 'refreshing'. She was educated to the Arya Samaj ideals and was happy to participate in the system which inculcated in her new religious values. Apart from Gujarati she also studied English, Hindi and Sanskrit. A strictly vegetarian diet was followed. The daily programme called for rising at 5 a.m. The girls were expected to perform a havan (fire ceremony) before proceeding to early morning exercises. Each girl was given a sacred thread (chonai) to signify her initiation into Hindu life. This initiation signified her rejection of the caste system and the following of a disciplined Hindu life. The girls were expected to chant verses from the Vedas, which they learn in the religious education class.

Mrs. K.D. said that the visit to South Africa by a group of girl guides from the Arya Kanya Mahavidyalaya in 1934[15] was the source of her inspiration to join the school. Several other girls were similarly inspired. The visit was unique because it was the only time that a group of Indian students had visited South Africa to display their physical and gymnastic skills. Pt. Nardev says "The excellent display of items such as Indian club swimming, feats of Yoga āsanas, archery, daggerdrill and sword fighting, held large audiences spellbound and captivated their hearts."[16] Pt. Nardev also believes that "The Guides exerted tremendous influence in enhancing the prestige of Indian womanhood in this country."[17]

The popular Indian weekly magazine "Illustrated Weekly of India" focused on this school during the Arya Samaj Centenary celebrations.[18] The school was started in Etola, near Baroda, in 1925, and is now situated on a 25 hectare site in a suburb of Baroda. It is a residential public school for girls, based on the Gurukula system. Until 1950 it followed its own syllabus and awarded its own certificates. Later, it adopted Government-recognised courses. Special bursaries and other scholarships are granted to Adivasis, Harijans and other "backward and scheduled" castes. Girls of all castes and creeds study there. Mrs. K.D., like several of her friends was deeply appreciative of the opportunity she had of studying there in a free and 'emancipated' education system.

During 1983, the Arya Pratinidhi Sabha marked the centenary of Swami Dayananda's death with a series of meetings. One of the more significant of these, was that on which no less than sixty women members were ordained as priests. The movement has thus earned for itself the distinction of admitting a large group of ordained ministers dedicated to the task of community service. The women now joined by many others, constitute the organisation known as the Maha Mahila Swadhyaya Mandal, which requires them to become committed to intensive study and propagation of the religious message of the Arya Samaj. The organisation encourages the holding of study groups, which are very popular. As ordained members they hope to revive the religious spirit which has been neglected for some time. Upon enrolling as members of the Swadhyaya Mandal they are asked to enter into a contract known as a *Vrata Grahanam*, by which they pledge themselves to spread the message of the Vedas, to always act in accordance with Vedic teachings, to study religious books and to do the work of the Sabha as a sacred duty.

Mrs. B.G. was interviewed as to the reasons for her enthusiastic association with the Arya Pratinidhi Sabha. She said she was drawn into the organisation through her local association with the Sarasvati Mahila Mandal, which encouraged women living in a southern suburb of Durban to meet for the purpose of conducting religious services. She was appointed as a delegate to meetings of the Arya Pratinidhi Sabha and she soon found her commitment to the cause growing.

Her commitment arises from her realisation of the serious need for more lay preachers to minister to the community. The problem of conversion to other religions she regarded as serious, so her dedication to the work of the Arya Pratinidhi Sabha arose from her desire to participate in the work of the Sabha.

The strongest feelings arise from the fact that, had it not been for the Arya Samaj, "we women would not have been emancipated". "We might have had to stay in purdah and be kept in ignorance", she says. "Because of the Arya Samaj we have been given our rightful place in life. And today we women play a very active part in cultural activities. In fact today we are the leaders in some of the fields. Thanks to the Arya Samaj for this."

Mrs. A.M. admitted readily to being upset about one specific feature of the teachings of the Arya Samaj. She was of the view that while Vedic teachings were responsible for bringing the attention of women to the glory of the teachings of Hinduism, a shift in emphasis from the epics and purāṅas had one unfortunate feature, namely loss of familiarity with the lives of some of the great women of Sanskrit literature. Even though Swami Dayananda may have had difficulties with the epics, particularly the purāṇas, she felt that, although they were purely literary figures, there was a portrayal of greatness in the lives of the great women of the *Rāmāyaṇa*, *Mahābhārata* and other works. She was of the view that Valmiki, the ascetic, for example, wrote his *Rāṁāyaṇa* fully aware of the importance of tapas (austerity), and swādhyāya (study of Vedas). She considered that it was never Valmiki's intention, nor Vyasa's either, to replace the Vedas with books of their authorship. All they did was to add a very human touch to Hindu culture by extolling the lives of some of the great women such as Sītā, Draupadi, Gandhārī and others. In more recent times Meera and even Sārada Devi, wife of Sri Ramakrishna, were not without their qualities of greatness, however much they may have differed theologically from Arya Samaj principles. Kalidasa's *Shakuntala* exemplified Indian femininity to the extent that few Arya Samaj ideas could, so she had to be emulated by Hindu women in all parts of the world. Although she was not familiar with the biographies of women who rose to high levels of attainment outside these works she was aware of great women in both North and South India. And if women in South Africa could be reminded of these heroic figures in both their religious and secular life some inspiration would emanate therefrom for their religious guidance.

REFERENCES

1. Behr, A.L. and MacMillan, B.C., *Education in South Africa.*
2. *Ibid.*, p 335.
3. *Ibid.*, p 336.
4. Rambiritch, B., *An Investigation into Some Aspects of the Education of Indian Girls in Natal*, University of Natal, Durban, 1955.
5. Rambiritch, B., *Ibid.*
6. Rambiritch, B., *Ibid.*
7. Rambiritch, B., *Ibid.*
8. Rambiritch, B., *Ibid.*
9. Kuper, H., *Indian People in Natal*, Greenwood Press, Westport, 1974.
10. Kuper, H., *Ibid.*
11. Kuper, H., *Ibid.*
12. Greyling, J.J.C., *Employment Opportunities for University Trained Indians*, Institute of Social and Economic Records, University of Durban-Westville, Durban, 1977.
13. University of Durban-Westville Records ST 4/1.
14. Greyling J.J.C., *Ibid.*, p 64.
15. Vedalankar, N., *Ibid.*, p 55.
16. Vedalankar, N., *Ibid.*, p 55.
17. Vedalankar, N., *Ibid.*, p 55.
18. *The Illustrated Weekly of India:* 13 April, 1975.

CHAPTER 4

Equality and Justice for All

DURING 1983, the Arya Pratinidhi Sabha attempted to focus attention on several aspects of its commitment to religious values. The feature of its activities for the year centred around the death of Swami Dayananda. One of the most notable meetings held during the year was that which the Chief Minister of KwaZulu, a member of the Zulu royal family, was feted. Among the reasons given for conferring honour on the Zulu leader was recognition of its contribution to the cause of justice for all people in South Africa. Members of the Hindu and other Indian communities and also the Zulu community of Stanger were invited. In this show of solidarity between the Indian and Zulu peoples of Northern Natal, the meeting was aimed at demonstrating the feelings for human justice that the communities shared. The Chief Minister was given the title, *Rashtriya Pitā* ('Apostle of Peace').

The meeting came closer than any other in demonstrating the Sabha's concern for political, social and religious justice. At several of the meetings held during the year reference was made to the fact that the Arya Samaj movement subscribed to the principles of justice and liberty through its stated decalogue.

The seventh principle concerns love and justice and exhorts Aryans to conduct themselves in accordance with its prescriptions on love, righteousness and justice. The tenth principle calls for subordination and liberty and requests that men should subscribe to the laws calculated to promote the well-being of all.[1]

In an address to members of the Arya Samaj at its headquarters during the centenary year of the Samaj in 1975, the Prime Minister of Mauritius referred to the principles of democracy in society. He said: "We are tied down by natural and inseparable relations and our individual well-being is not at all conceivable, much less realisable, except through the well-being of others."[2]

It would appear from the principles advocated within the movement that for the religious norms to become functionally meaningful, patterns of action that would reflect well on the personality of the members of the movement in interaction and relationship, must take place. The Arya Samaj, however, does not strictly define or explain the pattern of action within a clearly enunciated mechanistic technique. The socially mediated experience in interaction with other persons results in the development of characteristic structures in which religious and social norms form an important component. In the Arya Samaj, reciprocal relationships function along a mode that rests heavily on situational standards, very much as Swami Dayananda did. He becomes therefore the model, as Parsons describes, for religious socialisation to become functional.[3]

In a newsletter published by the Arya Pratinidhi Sabha on 1 March 1983, several programmes were outlined that were to be observed during the course of the centenary year.[4] The members of the Samaj, have also been reminded that a hand of friendship was to be extended to all non-Hindus. Such solidarity should first be between all Hindus. In other words, discrimination practised within the community should end before expressions of friendship could be extended outside the community.

The birth of the Arya Pratinidhi Sabha was marked by a call among members of the Hindu community to display total commitment to the new approach to religious and more particularly social values by eradicating caste prejudices. At least five per cent of the Hindu community in South Africa were members of the Brahmin caste.[5] They were followed by other Brahmins later. Hilda Kuper, quoting from the Report of the Department of Revenue, Agriculture and Commerce of 1877, says that 21 per cent (some 628 persons) of the Hindu people who arrived in South Africa in 1875-6 were of high Brahmin caste.[6] Of the four language communities within the Hindu religious group in South Africa, the Hindi-speaking community have the largest number of members of the Brahmin caste. This heterogeneity among Hindu people tends to accentuate caste consciousness among them. Appreciation of this fact led to several steps being taken by the Arya Samaj movement to eradicate obvious problems. The reaction from caste Hindus was often vehement. But commitment to the ideals the Samaj set itself was one of the outstanding features of the movement. Now members of the Samaj, those holding the surname Mahārāj or Singh, feel proud of the fact that a former president of the Arya Pratinidhi Sabha belonged to the *śūdra* caste. Hilda Kuper correctly says that the caste system can only operate indirectly in South Africa, because the traditional view held by Indians in India is absent.[7] Despite this, the role played by the Arya Samaj in eliminating the system has been significant.

The integration of the individual persons into the social system depends on his acquisition of, and conformity to the cognitive and normative definitions of the group. This process of integration and adaptation to accept norms is a form of socialization which clearly spells out a code of conformity to Arya Samaj principles. The socialization includes a process of assimilation by the individual Arya Samajist to the cultural element defined by Dayananda but explained in local terms by Pandit Nardev and others within the movement. Socialization includes the whole process of assimilation with the local environment.

The prejudices that obtain within the community are particularly predominant within specific social and religious situations. Marriage is seldom contracted by parties across caste lines although this is changing. But at the time of the formation of the Arya Pratinidhi Sabha and for at least three decades thereafter the difficulties that obtained were not easily overcome. The influence of the Arya Samaj helped considerably to reduce prejudices by appealing to Hindus to adopt more open views on the matter.

The success achieved by the Arya Samaj has contributed to an increase in inter-caste marriages and has also resulted in a certain accentuation of the differences between the Arya Pratinidhi Sabha and another major Hindi religio-cultural organisation representative of the Hindi-speaking people in South Africa. Caste prejudices still exist today in considerably reduced measure. Appeals to the community to observe the rules of social equality has found much support and many members of the Arya Samaj movement now view with pride the success achieved in reducing caste prejudices while viewing with disdain the failure of others to reduce racial prejudices with equal earnestness.

REFERENCES

1. Ten Principles of Arya Samaj.
2. Ram Gulam, S., Presidential Address, Arya Pratinidhi Sahba, Durban, 1975.
3. Parsons, T., *The Social System*, Free Press, Illinois, 1949, p 211.
4. Newsletter, Dayananda, Arya Pratinidhi Sabha, Durban, 1983.
5. Kuper, H., *Indian People in Natal*, Greenwood Press, Westport, 1974.
6. Kuper, H., *Ibid.*
7. Kuper, H., *Ibid.*

SECTION SEVEN

CONCLUSION

An Interpretive Summary of the Mode of Influence of the Arya Samaj on Hinduism in South Africa

IN THIS CHAPTER we summarise our findings on the work of the Arya Samaj movement as a religious action system within South Africa's Hindu community. This interpretive summary discusses the mode of religious expression within the movement in terms of the superordinate meaningfulness defined by both its theoretical structure (with which we also discuss its cultural value) and its organisational structure which contributes to the influence its belief system has on Hinduism in South Africa.

THEORETICAL STRUCTURE

The Arya Samaj doctrine finds its highest level of expression in the teachings of Swami Dayananda Sarasvati. Its symbolism lies rooted in the Vedas, especially the Saṁhitās, which he regarded as revealed authority. The Vedas reflect the cognitive beliefs of all Arya Samajists, whose modes of belief and expression are intended to modify socio-cultural patterns of behaviour within modern Hinduism. The superordinate meaningfulness of the entire Arya Samaj doctrine lies in Vedic Truth, which the Samaj contends expresses its highest values in specific aspects of its doctrinal content. This doctrinal content is referred to as *Swamantavya-mantavya* which Swami Dayananda enumerated in his *Satyartha Prakash.*[1] The Samaj sees the Ṛg Veda, Yajur Veda, Sāma Veda and the Atharva Veda as being produced and revealed by the Supreme and Perfect Being, Para-Brahman, who possesses the attributes of Self-existence, Consciousness and Bliss. Who is also Omnipotent and universally adored.[2]

The Vedic symbolism is further extended in the endeitic relation that man has with the highest concept of Truth and Supreme Happiness. Within the Arya Samaj, attempts are made to understand the philosophical implications of the teachings advocated but the movement functions within a limited sphere of conceptual discourse. However, basic teachings on God, salvation and the purpose of worship are given.[3]

Swami Dayananda's ethical system is underlined by his belief in Dharma as the practice of equitable justice together with that of truthfulness in action.

The concept of Saṁskāras takes on a modified significance within the movement in South Africa. The teachings are given with emphasis on particular tenets which find favour with conceptual modes in places such as the orphanage and old age home.

The superordinate objectives within the Arya Samaj such as Vedic Truth, Om, Śuddhī, Brahmacarya and service to man, reflect on situations within the movement. These form the core of the spiritual symbolism found within the Samaj and bear out what Saksena[4] regards as, not a mystic religion, but a mode of life that gives Hindusim an accentuated ethos. They in fact guide and sustain the true religiosity on which the movement is based. For Arya Samajists living in South Africa, far removed from the Indian situation, their symbols of religious conceptualisation are bulwarks of religious affiliation which sanctify religious behaviour and belief. Eliade[5] observes that this underlies the existential values of religious symbolism which opens up levels of religious reality that would otherwise remain closed to any form of commitment, much less meaning. Thus the superordinate meaningfulness of the Arya Samaj movement translates for Arya Samajists in particular and many Hindus in general, their human, cultural situation into the cosmological terms implied by the ancient faith they follow. The devotees thus became assured of the whole 'point' of religious affiliation and commitment and the total movement comes alive in more meaningful ways than many have been able to find in other forms of worship.

CULTIC VALUE

Closely allied to the teachings of Swami Dayananda are the principles on which the Arya Samaj movement was formed. "His creation, the Arya Samaj, postulates as principle, equal justice for all men and all nations, together with equality of the sexes."[6] This equality, it would appear, is built on the act of purification and ennoblement which the Samaj in South Africa has accepted as the means for its spiritual growth. Pandit Nardev[7] says that worship is a useful means of purifying and ennobling life. Such worship frees man from sin and pollution and from it follows every form of religious endeavour.

Dayananda's thesis of action and creed of battle were obviously formulated by his day-to-day experience of the wickedness he saw all around him. From this arose the serious intention to institute reforms in society. The whole purpose of prayer and participation in every religious act is directed at "the well-being of mankind as a whole", which "ought to be the objective of the Samaj."[8] We shall consider these objectives and their attainments in the following section.

The Arya Samaj has adopted a standard form of religious service which each centre maintains, if possible. Each service begins with invocation, followed by Sandhyā, Havan, a sermon and Śānti Pāth. Services focus on the act of worship and the principles Swami Dayananda sought to inculcate into the minds of his followers. Dedication to the work of the founding fathers is emphasized. Ethical discipline is stressed and includes *Tapas* (austerity), *Satyam* (truth) and *Śāntam* (peace). Truth is, however, considered the Supreme Virtue.[9]

The virtues emphasized in every Arya Samaj service form the basis of religious belief which enables the congregation to conceptualise the paramount importance of religious integration. The havan ceremony, accompanied by sermonic dialogue, is the heart of religious practice. In most services members of the congregation pay little attention to the details concerning Vedic eschatology or soteriology. However much Swami Dayananda's teachings may be distinctive, thus providing the basis for the features that distinguish Arya Samaj theology, members are content to participate in worship for the religious satisfaction that emanates from its every act. The manner in which worship is undertaken is a unique form of systematization of worship which emanates largely from Swami Dayananda's work as an innovator of religious reintegration. Thus the sacred objects such as havan give symbolic representation to worship with the emphasis on sacred virtues as a point of convergence between the act of worship and religious conceptualisation.

Our study of the Arya Pratinidhi Sabha and Arya Samaj as a broader classification brings into focus the sect-cult type of religious institution. It holds to the ideals of perfection based upon love and service and a lasting fellowship among its members. It reveals the characteristics of a sect in emphasizing the ideal of perfection and religious growth. The goal for the Arya Samaj therefore does not lie in bringing salvation to the individual within the framework of a movement such as the Sabha but allows its universal principles to infiltrate into the wider spectrum of religious developments for Hinduism and if possible beyond it.

Loomis[10] says that religious action through the use of sacred objects offers a concrete reference for the values emphasized within the system. This accentuates a sense of belonging and contributes greatly to the enhancement of religious commitment.

In so doing, the Pundits conducting the service share in the integrative function of worship. Worship serves the function of renewal of faith while religious symbols serve the task of reaffirming the integrative role of worship. In this way faith is maintained or restored. The personality of Dayananda and his suffering, serve as the motivating force for greater commitment. The life of Swami Dayananda plays an integrative role symbolising the underlying faith necessary for religious reinforcement. Ritual then becomes a way of producing religious service. This ideal is never in want of teaching by example because many other aspects of the work of the Arya Samaj remind the congregation of the binding wholeness of religious solidarity found within the movement in its wide areas of service.

SAMAJIC INFLUENCE ON SOUTH AFRICAN HINDUISM: ORGANISATIONAL STRUCTURE

The institutions affiliated to the Arya Pratinidhi Sabha bear the weight of the work the Sabha has undertaken in the name of religious endeavour. Arya Samajists emphasize how much they are a part of a wider community so they direct their energies to influencing the community as a whole in every aspect of Hindu religious practice. Taking its cue from a view expressed by the leadership in India, members of the Samaj set about their tasks in numerous ways.[11]

The Veda Niketan, through its numerous publications, has spread the message of Hinduism to every part of South Africa. A publication entitled "The Fundamental Teachings of Hinduism" has been distributed throughout the country and overseas, thus enabling the Samaj to influence Hindu thinking in the most positive way possible. A feature of this work is that although it expresses many ideas that the Arya Samaj considers important it also stresses the essentials of Hinduism of relevance to the South African Hindu community. In this respect many Hindus in South Africa thus became familiar with more tangible concepts of an ethical system having direct relevance to the South African situation.

For example, Swami Dayananda's ethical system is underlined by his belief in Dharma as the practice of equitable justice together with that of truthfulness in thought, word and deed. He emphasizes, however, that ethical disciplines have to conform with Divine Will as embodied in the Vedas. Only righteously acquired wealth constitutes *artha*, while all other forms of wealth constitute *anartha*. The enjoyment of legitimate desires with the help of honestly acquired wealth constitutes *kāma*. While the concepts are understood among Hindus generally, Dayananda's emphasis and more particularly the Arya Samajic presentation of them to Hindus in South Africa, help to reformulate religious growth in the community. Consider Dayananda's views concerning marriage and the Samaj's attempt to reformulate the traditional conceptions of it for the benefit of members of the Hindu community. Marriage he regards as the union of a man and woman through mutual consent in accordance with the laws laid down by the Vedas. Niyoga, in accordance with ancient practice, is a temporary union for the raising of children. The part Arya Samaj has been able to play in the lives of many Hindus in South Africa in this regard is significant because of its ability to unite families from different linguistic backgrounds. When a member of the Hindu community marries a member of another language group, an Arya Samaj wedding helps to circumvent numerous problems arising from the specific customary rituals necessary for either party. Since the formation of the Vedic Purohit Mandal and the building of the Vedic Temple, numerous changes have been instituted in the way Hindu weddings are performed for the entire Hindu community. The emphasis placed upon simplicity of belief and ritualistic practice has modified approaches to ritualism within the Hindu community to the extent that a considerable proportion of Hindi and many non-Hindi speaking people now appreciate their value.

The Samaj's ritualistic scheme is now seen as an innovation of considerable importance and consequence for the community as a whole and is increasingly being appreciated. This influence is also spreading due to the growth in the number of priests in the organisation. In this way, it is able to emphasize its views concerning the performance of Saṁskāras, rites which contribute to the physical, mental and spiritual well-being of man. Saṁskāras have to be performed as an obligatory, ritualistic duty.[12] The most significant contribution to this branch of religious practice by the Arya Samaj, however, lies in its view that no ritual need be performed for the departed after cremation. This is a matter of considerable discussion among Hindus and while the controversy rages, the Arya Samaj viewpoint on the matter gains ground increasingly.

The Arya Samaj has contributed one ritual practice that is growing in popularity and importance among Hindu communities throughout the country. The Agnihotra or havan ceremony is being performed increasingly with greater numbers of people becoming interested in it as a medium for religious expression. Its importance lies in its implication as an act of purification in which God is invoked through fire—one of the primordial elements. Apart from personal purification as an act of worship, it purifies the air, the vegetables and plants and directly promotes the well-being of all sentient creatures. The performance of *Yajña* (scarifice) and the resort of *Tīrthas* (sacred places) are, however, lifted from the realm of rituals to that of the moral ideal. Yajña for the Arya Samajists consists of showing due respect to the wise and the learned, for in its performance lies the invocation and the supplication as well as the intercession for and on behalf of all fellow beings, the earth, the interspace, the animals, the plants and all the living beings of the world. This is followed by an intercession of spiritual growth resulting from a study of scripture, science, the arts and all other knowledge. Tīrthas, the means by which the ocean of misery is crossed, consists in the practice of truthfulness in speech, in the acquisition of true knowledge, in the cultivation of the habits of associating with the wise and performing deeds that are commendable.

The institution of religious examinations by the Veda Niketan has enabled it to become responsible for hundreds of students becoming familiar with the essentials of Hinduism in a way no other Hindu organisation has so far been able to emulate. Students in many parts of the country now participate in the annual examinations and thereby become aware of the influence the Arya Samaj movement has on Hinduism in this country.

Although the work of the Aryan Benevolent Home does not feature as religious work, its religious connotations indicate the karma yoga discipline. People associate the philanthropic work of the home with the essential religious calling of the Arya Samaj and in this way the Samaj's message spreads and becomes well-known among many people.

The Arya Pratinidhi Sabha's establishment of Hindi schools is recognised as an act of service to young people who, during youth camps and other outings, come to understand what Arya Samaj principles are and eventually find themselves adapting to a new form of Hinduism free of many ritualistic practices and, above all, free of caste prejudices. In this respect the Arya Samaj is recognised as an institution of reform that introduced a new religious system which sacrifices nothing of the sublime in Hindu ethical or theological doctrine. Its Vedic temple still symbolises the best in religious endeavour and keeps Hinduism vibrant in many ways.

Despite the arduous nature of the functions carried out by the Sabha in South Africa in the face of exacting social conditions, the charismatic personality of its leader Swami Dayananda appears as one of the chief motivating factors of its development. The example set by him has led many in the organisation to commit themselves to acts of service, thus following the lead of what Weber calls "exemplary prophecy", i.e. showing others the road to salvation by personal example of suffering and service and finally the teaching of religious truth.

The structural changes initiated by Swami Dayananda in the organisational framework of religious institutionalisation have struck a significant cord within the Hindu movement. The Samaj speaks of revitalising Hinduism by eliminating aspects of social ethics such as the caste system. It also inculcates new life into Hinduism by emphasizing the principles of universal brotherhood. The Arya Pratinidhi Sabha thus emphasises fundamental elements of religious practice as conceived by it, to enhance its reputation independent of the charismatic personality that was its original inspiration.

South Africa having given birth to three well-known Hindu religious institutions in the years following the birth of the Arya Pratinidhi Sabha, lends itself to religious conceptualisation in a way that does not reject age-old patterns of worship however much these may be regarded as neither useful nor necessary in the long term. But the Arya Pratinidhi Sabha (following a useful line of service which is strengthened by visits to this country by eminent Samajists) is appreciated by a vast number of Hindus.

The ten principles the Arya Samaj adopted in India form a focal point of religious commitment by Arya Samajists in South Africa. The need for a doctrinal basis is clearly recognised by many people who also appreciate its directional influence. Religion for Arya Samajists is not an exclusive individual affair. "We are not isolated beings obviously put together by some external agency. We are tied down by natural and inseparable relations and our individual well-being is not all conceivable, much less realisable except through the well-being of others." For this reason, Arya Samaj rejects the caste system and decrees that all Hindus, irrespective of caste, shall study the Vedas. It begins its scheme of work by emphasizing the necessity for worship to be conducted systematically and methodically and also contends that all worship shall be arranged in accordance with a fundamental set of principles. Since the inception of the Sabha many Hindu organisations have been influenced into formulating their own systems of worship according to regulated patterns.

The Sabha, in emphasizing its desire to uphold Arya Samaj principles, rejects such doctrines as that of the *Avatāra*. It vehemently condemns idolatry and also condemns the practice of animal sacrifice or even offering food at the altar to God. It also disapproves of the ancient custom of ancestor worship as it does the idea that pilgrimage to a holy shrine has any spiritual value.

These practices form an important focus of attention among Arya Samajists because the attempt at reform is aimed directly at practices the Samaj regards as having no religious or cultural meaningfulness. The attempt therefore to proselytise its message meets with some resistance, which does not necessarily arise through direct opposition but rather fear of parting from old and time-honoured practices. The message of the Arya Samaj travels a long and difficult road, meeting with orthodoxy and nebulousness among older people while younger ones receive it sympathetically and at times with open enthusiasm.

The Arya Pratinidhi Sabha labours under difficulties it shares with religious movements world-wide born within and outside the fold of Hinduism. It functions through clearly defined motives and aims at achieving goals of far-reaching consequence for the Hindu community nationally. The nature of its work and philosophy encourages an inherent dynamism that occasionally slackens under the strain of economic, social and political pressures. However, numerous affiliated institutions which support the many faceted attack on religious conservatism and short-sighted orthodoxy sustain its steady growth. As an institution of service it stands to gain if it vigorously searches out and develops the ideas that enhance its contribution to the growth and development of the community as a whole. Its message is quite clearly being appreciated in widening areas of community life, not only as means for personal salvation but also as a gift of service of lasting religious enhancement and involvement.

REFERENCES

1. Sarda, H.B., *Life of Dayanand*, p. 224.
2. Sarda, H.B., *Ibid*, p. 426.
3. Sarma, D.S., *Hinduism through the Ages*, p. 92.
4. Saksena, R.N., *Society Social Research and Social Religious Symbolism*, p. 8.
5. Eliade, M., *Methodological Remarks on the Study of Religious Symbolism*, p. 102.
6. Rolland, R., *The Life of Ramakrishna*, p. 143.
7. Vedalankar, N., *Aryan Prayer*, p. 7.
8. Rolland, R., *Ibid.*, p. 142.
9. Satyaprakash, S., *Outlines of Vedic Philosophy*, p. 212.
10. Loomis, C.P., *Social Systems*, p. 210.
11. *Arya Samaj at a Glance*, Sarvadeshik Arya Sabha, Delhi, 1975.
12. Jordens, *Ibid.*

Glossary

Ācārya	:	A Religious teacher
Agnihotra	:	Fire ceremony involving the offering of oblations
Āryavarta	:	Another name for India
Bhīl	:	A mountain tribesman
Brahmacarya	:	A student
Brahman	:	The Impersonal, formless Supreme Being
Brahmin	:	A member of the priestly community
Devatās	:	Deities
Dharma	:	Religious law
Gṛhastha āśrama	:	Householders's station in life
Gurukula	:	A school, the guru's place for study
Harijan	:	Child of God; a member of a scheduled caste
Kanṭhi	:	A stringed neckband
Kśatriya	:	A warrior; a member of the military community
Pāṭhśālā	:	A school
Parabrahman	:	The Supreme Brahman
Parivrājaka	:	Wandering monk
Pūjā	:	Worship
Sanatana Dharma	:	The Eternal Faith
Sanatani	:	A follower of Sanatana Dharma
Sandhyā	:	Twilight prayers
Saṁskāra	:	Holy sacrament
Satyam	:	Truth
Śāligrām	:	A stone image; an idol
Śāntam	:	Peace
Śāstrārtha	:	A discussion on holy scripture
Śilpavidyā	:	The science and technology of architecture
Śivālaya	:	Temple dedicated to Lord Śiva
Śuddhī	:	A purification ceremony
Snātaka	:	A graduate of a school
Śūdra	:	A member of the labouring caste
Swadeshi	:	Goods manufactured locally
Swarāj	:	Home rule; independence
Tapas	:	Austerities
Tilak	:	A mark on the forehead

Upāsanā	: Prayer or meditation
Vaiśya	: A member of the business caste
Vamamārgism	: 'Leftist' practice
Vedālaṅkār and Vidyālaṅkār	: Degrees conferred by Gurukul University and other oriental Institutions.
Vidyārthī	: A student
Yajñopavīta	: Sacred thread worn by Brahmin and the twice born

Index